T0269883

Halloween

This book argues that *Halloween* need not be the first nor the most influential youth slasher film for it to hold a special place in the history of youth cinema.

John Carpenter's 1978 horror hit was once considered the be-all, end-all of teen slasher cinema and was regarded as the first, the best, and the most influential American slasher film. Recent revisions in film history, however, have challenged *Halloween*'s comfortable place in the canon of youth horror cinema. However, this book argues that the film, like no other, draws from the themes, imagery, and obsessions that fueled youth horror cinema since the 1950s—Gothic atmosphere, atomic dread, twisted psychology, and alienated teenage monsters—and ties them together in the deceptively simple story of a masked killer on Halloween night. Along the way, the film delivers a savage critique of social institutions and their failure to protect young people. *Halloween* also depicts a cadre of compelling and complicated youth characters: teenage babysitters watching over preadolescents as a killer, who is viciously avoiding the responsibilities of young adulthood, stalks them through the shadows.

This book explores all these aspects of *Halloween*, including the franchise it spawned, providing an invaluable insight into this iconic film for students and researchers alike.

Mark Bernard is Assistant Professor of English at Siena Heights University. His primary research interests are horror cinema and media industries. He is the author of *Selling the Splat Pack: The DVD Revolution and the American Horror Film*.

Cinema and Youth Cultures
Series Editors: Siân Lincoln & Yannis Tzioumakis

Cinema and Youth Cultures engages with well-known youth films from American cinema as well as the cinemas of other countries. Using a variety of methodological and critical approaches the series volumes provide informed accounts of how young people have been represented in film, while also exploring the ways in which young people engage with films made for and about them. In doing this, the Cinema and Youth Cultures series contributes to important and long standing debates about youth cultures, how these are mobilized and articulated in influential film texts and the impact that these texts have had on popular culture at large.

The Virgin Suicides
Justin Wyatt

The Breakfast Club
Elissa H. Nelson

The Freshman
Christina G. Petersen

Y Tu Mamá También
Scott L. Baugh

Halloween
Mark Bernard

American Pie
Bill Osgerby

For more information about this series, please visit: www.routledge.com/
Cinema-and-Youth-Cultures/book-series/CYC

Halloween
Youth Cinema and the Horrors of Growing Up

Mark Bernard

Routledge
Taylor & Francis Group

LONDON AND NEW YORK

First published 2020 by Routledge

2 Park Square, Milton Park, Abingdon, Oxon OX14 4RN
605 Third Avenue, New York, NY 10017

Routledge is an imprint of the Taylor & Francis Group, an informa business

First issued in paperback 2021

Library of Congress Cataloging-in-Publication Data
Names: Bernard, Mark, author.
Title: Halloween : youth cinema and the horrors of growing up /
    Mark Bernard.
Description: London ; New York : Routledge, 2020. | Series: Cinema and
    youth cultures | Includes bibliographical references and index.
Identifiers: LCCN 2019029189 (print) | LCCN 2019029190 (ebook) |
    ISBN 9781138732407 (hardcover) | ISBN 9781315185453 (ebook)
Subjects: LCSH: Halloween (Motion picture : 1978) | Halloween films. |
    Youth in motion pictures. | Slasher films—United States—History and
    criticism. | Horror films—United States—History and criticism.
Classification: LCC PN1997.H25836 B47 2020 (print) |
LCC PN1997.H25836 (ebook) | DDC 791.43/75—dc23
LC record available at https://lccn.loc.gov/2019029189
LC ebook record available at https://lccn.loc.gov/2019029190

ISBN: 978-1-138-73240-7 (hbk)
ISBN: 978-1-03-217705-2 (pbk)
DOI: 10.4324/9781315185453

Typeset in Times New Roman
by Apex CoVantage, LLC

Dedicated with love to Hope Bernard, who walked with me—literally and figuratively—through the streets of Haddonfield.

Frontispiece: *Halloween*, 1978. Director: John Carpenter

Image courtesy of Falcon International/Kobal/Shutterstock

Contents

Figures

Series Editors' Introduction

Despite the high visibility of youth films in the global media marketplace, especially since the 1980s when Conglomerate Hollywood realized that such films were not only strong box office performers but also the starting point for ancillary sales in other media markets as well as for franchise building, academic studies that focused specifically on such films were slow to materialize. Arguably the most important factor behind academia's reluctance to engage with youth films was a (then) widespread perception within the Film and Media Studies communities that such films held little cultural value and significance, and therefore were not worthy of serious scholarly research and examination. Just like the young subjects they represented, whose interests and cultural practices have been routinely deemed transitional and transitory, so were the films that represented them perceived as fleeting and easily digestible, destined to be forgotten quickly, as soon as the next youth film arrived in cinema screens a week later.

Under these circumstances, and despite a small number of pioneering studies in the 1980s and early 1990s, the field of 'youth film studies' did not really start blossoming and attracting significant scholarly attention until the 2000s and in combination with similar developments in cognate areas such as 'girl studies.' However, because of the paucity of material in the previous decades, the majority of these new studies in the 2000s focused primarily on charting the field and therefore steered clear of long, in-depth examinations of youth films or was exemplified by edited collections that chose particular films to highlight certain issues to the detriment of others. In other words, despite providing often wonderfully rich accounts of youth cultures as these have been captured by key films, these studies could not have possibly dedicated sufficient space to engage with more than just a few key aspects of youth films.

In more recent (post-2010) years a number of academic studies started delimiting their focus and therefore providing more space for in-depth examinations of key types of youth films, such as slasher films and biker films or examining youth films in particular historical periods. From that point on, it was a matter of time for the first publications that focused exclusively on key youth films from a number of perspectives to appear (*Mamma Mia! The Movie*, *Twilight* and *Dirty Dancing* are among the first films to receive this treatment). Conceived primarily as edited collections, these studies provided a multifaceted analysis of these films, focusing on such issues as the politics of representing youth, the stylistic and narrative choices that characterize these films and the extent to which they are representative of a youth cinema, the ways these films address their audiences, the ways youth audiences engage with these films, the films' industrial location and other relevant issues.

It is within this increasingly maturing and expanding academic environment that the **Cinema and Youth Cultures** volumes arrive, aiming to consolidate existing knowledge, provide new perspectives, apply innovative methodological approaches, offer sustained and in-depth analyses of key films and therefore become the 'go to' resource for students and scholars interested in theoretically informed, authoritative accounts of youth cultures in film. As editors, we have tried to be as inclusive as possible in our selection of key examples of youth films by commissioning volumes on films that span the history of cinema, including the silent film era; that portray contemporary youth cultures as well as ones associated with particular historical periods; that represent examples of mainstream and independent cinema; that originate in American cinema and the cinemas of other nations; that attracted significant critical attention and commercial success during their initial release and that were 'rediscovered' after an unpromising initial critical reception. Together these volumes are going to advance youth film studies while also being able to offer extremely detailed examinations of films that are now considered significant contributions to cinema and our cultural life more broadly.

We hope readers will enjoy the series.

Siân Lincoln & Yannis Tzioumakis
Cinema & and Youth Cultures Series Editors

Acknowledgments

I would like to thank Siân Lincoln and Yannis Tzioumakis for inviting me to write this volume for this series. I appreciate their kindness, guidance, and patience during the writing process. Special thanks to the amazing Kim Gottlieb-Walker for generously allowing me to use one of her photos. Thanks also to Marcus Alexander Hart at OldPalMarcus.com for allowing me to use his handy flowchart. This book would not have been possible without previous scholarship by the late Peter Hutchings, Murray Leeder (thanks for the extra tidbit from your interview with Carpenter, Murray), Richard Nowell, Timothy Shary, Andrew Tudor, and the late Robin Wood. Special thanks to them. Thanks to everyone in the Humanities Division at Siena Heights University for their support and encouragement. Finally, thanks to Cynthia Baron, Colin Helb, Greg Simpson, and Jenn and Callie (again) for talking me off the ledge, whether they knew they were doing it or not.

Introduction

It is Halloween night in Haddonfield, Illinois. As autumn leaves float through the air, teenager Laurie Strode (Jamie Lee Curtis) sits on the stoop in front of her house with a pumpkin on her lap, waiting for her friend Annie Brackett (Nancy Loomis) to pick her up for a ride to their babysitting gigs (see Figure 0.1). When Annie pulls up, Laurie waddles across the street with the pumpkin and gets in. During the drive, the two discuss their plans for the night. Laurie intends to carve a pumpkin with Tommy Doyle (Brian Andrews), while Annie foresees a night in front of the television for herself and Lindsey Wallace (Kyle Richards). She says, 'I plan on making popcorn and watching Doctor Dementia. Six straight hours of horror movies. Little Lindsey Wallace won't know what hit her.' Later, Laurie and Tommy also eventually opt for some television, as the film later shows them sitting on the couch at the Doyle residence and watching a broadcast of *The Thing from Another World* (Nyby and Hawks, 1951). Across the street at the Wallace residence, Lindsey also watches *The Thing* as Annie connives to ditch Lindsey and pick up her boyfriend Paul. Annie dumps

Figure 0.1 Laurie waits for a ride

Lindsey on Laurie and leaves for a date, but she will not even make it out of the driveway. Michael Myers (Nick Castle), an escaped maniac, attacks Annie in her car, strangling her and slitting her throat. Back at the Doyle house, the kids watch *Forbidden Planet* (Wilcox, 1956) as Doctor Dementia's marathon continues.

These scenes from *Halloween*, the 1978 low-budget sleeper that would soon become a staple of both youth and horror cinema, feature adolescents and preadolescents watching films from the 1950s targeted at youth audiences. During the 1950s, young people became the dominant audience for the movies, thus sending the 'adult minds' of Hollywood execs 'racing madly to interpret adolescent tastes' (Doherty 2002: 132). In some ways, *Halloween* is this type of youth movie. The basic scenario of the film—suburban teenager babysitters stalked by a mad killer—was conceived by the 'adult mind' of Irwin Yablans, the head of Compass International, a small independent producer and distributor. Yablans, an industry veteran who had been working in the movie business in various capacities since the 1950s (Nichols 1980: 42), believed the concept for the film, tentatively titled 'The Babysitter Murders,' was a perfect fit for youth audiences: 'It occurred to me that if we did a movie about babysitters, it would . . . lend itself to kids in jeopardy' (Anchor Bay 2013b). To realize his vision, Yablans employed John Carpenter, a young writer/director whose previous film, the low-budget action thriller *Assault on Precinct 13* (1976), had been distributed in the US by Yablans's previous distribution company, Turtle Films. Carpenter was set to direct and co-write the film with his partner, Debra Hill, who would also produce. With this creative team in hand, Yablans convinced financier Moustapha Akkad to put up the film's budget, assuring him the film would be marketable to youth audiences (Nowell 2011: 81).

Although the germ of the film's concept came from an adult mind, *Halloween* was brought to fruition by a young cast and crew. In the 1950s, production companies ranging from the big studios to tiny independents made films geared for youth audiences. However, those teenpics made by independent production companies like American International Pictures (AIP) resonated with youth audiences because they felt like 'the kind of motion pictures a group of high schoolers let loose with 35 mm equipment might come up with, an impression due in equal parts to market savvy, youthful talent, and bargain-basement budgets' (Doherty 2002: 132). *Halloween* embodied all the characteristics of the best independent teenpics of the 1950s and 1960s. It not only featured youth characters, but was also driven by a youthful ethos behind the camera, truly a film made for young people, by young people. The marketable idea at the heart of the film was brought to life by a young cast and crew forced to be innovative due to time and money restrictions. After hiring Carpenter and Hill, Yablans realized no one had made a horror film based around the Halloween holiday, so he suggested Carpenter and Hill re-name the film *Halloween* and have the film take place on the holiday, changes that would potentially make the film even more marketable and appealing to young people. Hill agreed, later recalling, 'The Halloween theme was just a perfect theme. . . . [It] enabled us to . . . really plant ourselves in a teenage world' (Anchor Bay 2013a).

By all accounts, the youthful attitude of the teenage world was not limited to the diegesis. Looking back on the production, Carpenter described *Halloween*'s cast and crew as a 'little army' consisting of 'a bunch of kids trying to make a movie' (Anchor Bay 2013b). Curtis, who rose to stardom after the film's release, later recalled the production as being

> like guerilla movie-making. It was done on such a low budget. . . . Everybody was very young. I think John and Debra were the oldest people on the set. They were thirty. So, there were all these young grips and young electricians and young actors. . . . It was just really a magical time.
>
> (Anchor Bay 2013a)

As Hill recalls, 'We were kids back then in '78. People were giving us money. We were going out and playing. We had a huge sandbox to play in' (Anchor Bay 2013b). By Hollywood standards, *Halloween*'s sandbox was not that huge. The production budget was around $320,000, with principal photography taking place in various locations in South Pasadena and West Hollywood in April 1978 (Anchor Bay 2013b; Muir 2000: 13).[1]

Halloween rallies its limited resources to produce a simple, straightforward story. On Halloween night in 1963, 6-year-old Michael Myers (Will Sandin) brutally murders his teenage sister Judith (Sandy Johnson) with a butcher knife. Fifteen years later, in 1978, the now-adult Michael escapes from custody and returns to his hometown of Haddonfield, Illinois. In pursuit of Michael is Dr. Samuel Loomis (Donald Pleasence), Michael's former psychiatrist who is convinced that Michael is the embodiment of evil. Loomis warns Haddonfield's sheriff Leigh Brackett (Charles Cyphers) of the danger Michael poses to the little town, but it does not help. On Halloween night, Michael stalks and kills three teenagers: Annie, Lynda (P.J. Soles), and her boyfriend Bob (John Michael Graham). At the culmination of his killing spree, Michael attacks brainy teenager Laurie, who fights back but is unable to stop him. As Michael is about to strangle her, Loomis arrives on the scene and shoots Michael six times, sending him flying off the second-story balcony of a suburban home. However, when Loomis looks for Michael's body where it fell, he finds nothing. Michael has apparently walked away from a wounding that should have killed him, suggesting that Michael is an inhuman killing machine. Despite its humble beginnings, *Halloween* went on to gross around $47 million dollars domestically across several re-releases and spawned a franchise ('Franchises: Halloween' n.d.).[2]

Many histories cite *Halloween* as the genesis of what would come to be known as the teen slasher film,[3] a film-type that would dominate low-budget horror film production for the next few years, culminating in 1981, which saw the production of over 90 horror films, many of them low-budget slashers (Kendrick 2014: 311). Slasher films feature the basic formula of 'a blade-wielding killer preying on a group of young people' (Nowell 2011: 16). Using Rick Altman's semantic/syntactic approach to film genres, one could argue that the teen slasher combines semantic elements of the horror film—that is, the 'genre's building blocks'—with youth cinema's syntax, i.e. 'the structures into which [semantics] are arranged' (Altman 1999: 219).[4] Like many other slasher films, *Halloween* takes semantic elements from a range of previous horror texts and revises them for teen audiences. The Myers house, where young Michael killed his sister in 1963, is an update of the 'Terrible Place,' a generic component of Gothic literature dating back to the 18th century (Clover 2015: 80). Believed by neighborhood kids to haunted, the Myers house stands ominously among the well-kept homes of the American Midwest suburb of Haddonfield. In its depiction of Michael, a killer hailing from a banal, suburban environment, *Halloween* draws from the image of the human monster from mundane surroundings that had been relatively prevalent in horror cinema since *Psycho* (Hitchcock, 1960). Slashers usually take place in 'everyday surroundings' (Worland 2007: 227), syntactic structures that are 'almost always directly connected with the adolescent American experience in some way' (Kendrick 2014: 319). Reflecting the 'increasing awareness that the age of first intercourse was dropping for American youth' and American youth's growing interest in experimentation with drugs (Shary 2005: 55), the narratives of slasher movies were infused with sex and drugs, and the teenage victims of *Halloween* and many other slasher films to follow ran afoul of 'Terrible Places' and human monsters during their various pursuits of sex, alcohol, and illicit substances.

Over the past four decades, *Halloween* has been highly esteemed. It did not take very long for *Halloween* to become a 'canonical horror film' as it 'took its place in Film Studies . . . and remains a mainstay of horror classes' (Leeder 2014: 32). Popular critics like Gene Siskel and Roger Ebert offered *Halloween* as an example of a 'good' slasher film in contrast to other 'distasteful' teen slashers like *Friday the 13th* (Cunningham, 1980), *Prom Night* (Lynch, 1980), and *Terror Train* (Spottiswoode, 1980) (Nowell 2011: 226). Carpenter has grown into one of the most respected genre directors, with some discourses placing Carpenter among directors of the celebrated 'Hollywood Renaissance' alongside names like Martin Scorsese and Steven

Spielberg (Conrich and Woods 2004: 2–3). Although his career has been uneven from a commercial and critical viewpoint,[5] Carpenter nevertheless sits comfortably in the pantheon of 'great directors' and, in 2019, received the Golden Coach Award at the Cannes Film Festival Directors' Fortnight.

In 2018, the web series *Through the Lens*, produced by the Internet Movie Database and posted to its website, devoted an episode to Carpenter, titled 'Defining Carpenteresque.' The episode argued that the consistency of Carpenter's style and themes warrants his name being turned into an adjective, just as those of filmmakers such as Stanley Kubrick or David Lynch. Many film histories note Carpenter's auteur status, sometimes juxtaposing it with the downturn in quality of slasher films that followed *Halloween*. For instance, David Cook calls *Halloween* 'an artful, low-budget thriller' as opposed to the 'oafishly directed' *Friday the 13th*, a slasher blockbuster about teens stalked by an unseen killer at a summer camp that was released two years after *Halloween* (2016: 691). Over time, *Halloween* 'was commonly held up as the only creatively innovative teen slasher' (Nowell 2011: 9).

In recent years, however, *Halloween*'s comfortable position in the canon of horror cinema as the most prototypical, innovative, and influential slasher has been contested, with the most significant challenge coming from Richard Nowell. As Nowell argues, *Halloween* cannot lay claim to being the first slasher film. Instead, he cites *Black Christmas* (Clark, 1974), a low-budget, Canadian-made thriller, as the first slasher film and the film bearing the most influence over *Halloween* (2011: 57–78). While many past studies trace the slasher film's prehistory through films such as *Psycho* and *The Texas Chain Saw Massacre* (Hooper, 1974), Nowell maintains that these films actually bear little resemblance to what would come to be recognized as conventions of the slasher film, that is, 'a distinct setting, a shadowy killer, and a group of youths' (2011: 20). Also key to the slasher formula is a traumatic past event that triggers the killer (21). There are traces of these elements between *Psycho* and *The Texas Chain Saw Massacre*, but neither of these films delineates and organizes them into a recognizable slasher formula as clearly as *Black Christmas*, which offered a template that Yablans, Carpenter, and Hill followed when conceiving *Halloween* (57–79). Having called into question *Halloween*'s position as the first slasher film, Nowell chips away at *Halloween*'s nearly undisputed legacy as well, arguing that Carpenter's film is not the most influential and most imitated slasher film of the era. According to Nowell, this title would go to *Friday the 13th*. While *Friday the 13th* may be dismissed by Cook as 'oafishly directed,' Nowell points out that *Friday the 13th* not only kicked off the slasher boom of 1980 and 1981 but also more closely resembled the content of films that would follow during the first slasher cycle boom (120–147).

Regardless of these reasonable revisions to *Halloween*'s place in horror history, Carpenter's film remains a touchstone of horror and youth cinema for reasons that this monograph hopes to illuminate. If, as Nowell argues, *Friday the 13th*, not *Halloween*, was the most imitated slasher film of the era, then perhaps one may assume there are fewer slasher films like *Halloween* or even that Carpenter's film is unique among slasher films, possessing some traits and characteristics that most other slasher films—at least those from the first slasher cycle—do not. In his monograph dedicated to the film, Murray Leeder requests that the reader 'be content to acknowledge that *Halloween* is clearly related to the slasher cycle, but it is an entity distinct from it' (2014: 17). This book operates under a slightly different supposition: that *Halloween* is a significant youth horror film for reasons both related and unrelated to its affiliation with the slasher film subgenre.

To contextualize *Halloween* within the wider history of youth horror cinema, the first chapter offers an overview of youth horror's prehistory, its explosion in the 1950s, and its maturation in the 1960s and 1970s. When viewed in this context, *Halloween* emerges as a synthesis of youth horror's past thematic obsessions. Released at the end of the 1970s, the film emerged at a pivotal time in the late 1970s, when Hollywood was changing the way it did business. As such, if *Halloween* engages with youth horror's past, it also capitalizes on blockbuster filmmaking techniques and high concept marketing strategies that were emerging at the time of its release. Chapter 1 seeks to understand *Halloween* in its commercial context.

Halloween not only came along during a time of change for the Hollywood film industry, but it also emerged during a time when horror films were being taken more seriously and subjected to rigorous analysis in the academy. The second chapter begins by looking at how *Halloween* found itself in the middle of academic discourses and debates about the sociopolitical connotations of horror cinema. *Halloween* did not fare very well with critics like Robin Wood, who were disappointed with what they saw as the film's negligence to problematize the bourgeois patriarchal family via the figure of the monstrous child (Wood 1979a: 26). However, frameworks that deemphasize micro-psychoanalytic-based analysis in favor of macrosociological-based inquiry find that *Halloween* contains a potent critique of how social institutions have failed youth, leaving young people to wander in an inhospitable world.

The third chapter focuses on these youth characters and how they navigate through the rough terrain of childhood. Unlike most slasher films that focus solely on teenagers, *Halloween* offers an exploration of three different types of 'youth' characters: teenagers, preadolescents, and young adults. The chapter's analysis of the film's teen characters begins with a consideration of Laurie as the 'Final Girl,' a term coined by Carol J. Clover in her influential 1987 article 'Her Body, Himself: Gender in the Slasher Film' (Clover 2015). The Final Girl of the slasher film is the virginal young woman who, after all her friends are killed off, bests the killer and survives the ordeal. While classifying Laurie as a Final Girl is a fine way to begin an analysis of Laurie's character, the richness of *Halloween*'s depiction of youth begins to emerge when Laurie is considered in the context of the central trifecta of teen characters—Laurie, Annie, and Lynda—and how they resemble the archetypical teenage characters of the 'nerd,' the 'rebel, and the 'popular girl.' Preadolescents Tommy and Lindsey, the children Laurie and Annie are hired to babysit, also play a significant role in the film, especially Tommy, whose character trajectory shows how nonlinear the path from innocence to experience can be. Also overlooked in analyses of the film is the young adult category, as represented by the killer, Michael. It is tempting to read Michael as an overgrown kid stuck in a twisted perpetual childhood, but several indicators suggest Michael best fits into a category of young adult whose life has been derailed by a cruel, ineffective criminal justice system. Considering Michael in this light illuminates *Halloween*'s multifaceted depiction of youth cultures.

The final chapter provides an overview of the *Halloween* franchise including various sequels and remakes. *Halloween* has proven itself to be a durable franchise, even if the success of individual entries is often dependent of the state of the youth horror market at the time of their release. This chapter tracks how entries in the franchise produce a wide array of youth characters. The *Halloween* franchise focuses on trans-generational conflict and familial tension in a way that most other horror film franchises do not. While franchises like New Line's *Nightmare on Elm Street* series deal with familial tension between the young and the old, these conflicts often play out strictly between teenagers and their parents. The *Halloween* films also feature these clashes between the young and the old, but the franchise's representation of youth is more varied, as the films often feature characters like preadolescents in prominent roles. It has been a long time since an 18-year-old Laurie Strode sat on a stoop in the chilly October air, cradling a pumpkin and waiting for a ride. And it has been a long time since a group of young filmmakers sipped Dr Pepper and made horror film history in South Pasadena in 1978. But the film they made and the archetypical characters featured in that film possess eternal youth and vitality.

Notes

1 There are conflicting accounts when it comes to *Halloween*'s budget. Muir (2000: 13) and Boulenger (2001: 28) say the film's budget was $300,000. Nowell (2011: 81) cites Muir (2000: 13) as his source for *Halloween*'s budget but contradicts Muir's number and writes that the budget was $320,000. Yablans

(2012: 171) claims the budget was $325,000. I have chosen $320,000 because this is the figure that Joseph Wolf, one of the executives at Compass International, gives in Anchor Bay (2013b) and because this is the final figure Nowell settles on. Muir (2000: 14) is the source for the film's shooting schedule.

2 All box office figures and data refer to the US theatrical market and are taken from *Box Office Mojo*.
3 For example, see Dika (1990); Rockoff (2002); Worland (2007); Cook (2016).
4 See Nowell (2011) for a more nuanced discussion of the teen slasher film and genre theory.
5 For more about Carpenter's career, see Muir (2000); Boulenger (2001); Conrich (2019).

1 I Was a Teenage Psycho Killer

Halloween and the History of Youth Horror Cinema

Halloween's esteemed position in the history of youth horror cannot rely on it being the first teen slasher film. *Black Christmas* can more legitimately claim that title, not to mention the numerous proto-slasher films that predate both *Halloween* and *Black Christmas*, like *Psycho* and *The Texas Chain Saw Massacre*. Nor is *Halloween* the most influential slasher film; *Friday the 13th* offered a template more closely followed and imitated by future slasher films than that of *Halloween*. While John Carpenter's pedigree lends distinction to the film, *Halloween* is not the most highly regarded of Carpenter's films; judging by various fan and critical discourses, his 1982 remake of *The Thing* likely holds that title.[1]

This chapter argues that *Halloween* holds a privileged place in the history of youth horror because it offers a compendium of youth horror's past while looking toward its future. The film's plot is simple, adhering closely to unities of time, space, and action, but it also distills aspects of youth horror that made it so vital and exciting for several decades. Leeder identifies *Halloween* as 'one of the earliest horror films to depict characters *watching* horror films' (2014: 11), as youth horror's past is remediated on television with the broadcast of Doctor Dementia's Halloween movie marathon (see Figure 1.1). Scenes of preadolescents and teenagers watching 1950s-era youth horror on television invite the viewer to consider *Halloween* in the history of youth horror cinema. While *Halloween* does not utilize overt intertextuality to draw attention to youth horror film conventions and/or satirically comment on them, it does synthesize many facets of youth horror into a potent mix.

Halloween is usually credited for kicking off the first teen slasher boom, a trend that lasted until 1981, with the second cycle beginning in 1984. But what often remains underexplored is how the film fits into the overall evolution of horror and youth cinema.[2] Peter Hutchings (2013: 198–199) and Murray Leeder (2014: 73) have noted in passing the film's relationship with teenpics of the 1950s and 1960s. This chapter seeks to trace this

Figure 1.1 Tommy and Lindsey watch 'Doctor Dementia'

linage in more detail, contextualizing *Halloween* in the history of youth horror. Throughout the 1920s and 1930s, horror cinema was not associated with children's entertainment. It was not until the 1940s that the horror film courted youth audiences. The marketing of horror to teen audiences exploded in the 1950s, the golden age of youth horror, and there has been a significant relationship between youth and horror ever since.

This chapter looks at trends in youth horror that prefigured the thematic preoccupations of *Halloween*. Capturing the essence of youth horror's past, *Halloween* is a revamped 'weirdie,' the name given to that odd hybridization of horror and science fiction tailored for drive-in youth audiences of the 1950s (Doherty 2002: 119). *Halloween* also embodies the dark turn youth horror took in the 1960s and 1970s. While synthesizing youth horror's past, *Halloween* also looks toward its future, taking cues from contemporary blockbusters and signaling directions that both major studio and independent youth horror would take in the 1980s and 1990s. With this in mind, this chapter argues that, despite not being the first or most influential slasher film, *Halloween* nevertheless holds a privileged place in the history of horror cinema based on how it takes the disparate thematic threads of youth horror's history and deftly ties them together in an economically precise narrative. In the deceptively simple story of a killer stalking teenage victims on Halloween night, Carpenter employs elements of youth horror's past to great effect. More specifically, one can detect vestiges of the killer robot and atomic dread of 1950s sci-fi, the Gothic atmosphere of Hammer Films and AIP's Poe adaptations, the dark psychology and its attendant violence of 1960s horror (but without the gore), and the female leads meant to appeal to growing female audiences in the 1970s. Further, this chapter maintains that

Halloween was among the first low-budget, independent teenpics to employ blockbuster strategies that the major studios were in the process of adopting. Slick marketing made *Halloween* a youth horror brand name perfect for the multiplex era. As such, this chapter argues that *Halloween* is a culmination of three decades of drive-in youth horror and the beginning of youth horror during the age of the blockbuster.

A Brief Prehistory of Youth Horror

Horror cinema's origins mainly come from three sources: Gothic literature; the Grand Guignol Theatre founded in Paris in 1894, which showcased brief 'playlets' featuring gory violence; and traveling carnival sideshows which often featured 'freaks' and 'human oddities' (Dixon 2010: 22; Skal 1993: 29–30). All these influences come together in the German film *The Cabinet of Dr. Caligari* (Wiene, 1920), which tells the story of a carnival mountebank (Werner Krauss) who commands a somnambulist (Conrad Veidt) to do his evil bidding. *Caligari* was a product of German Expressionism, an artistic movement fueled by the Gothic's dark, symbolic settings and twisted psychology. When it was released in the US in 1921, *Caligari* was a critical sensation, influencing American cinema throughout the 1920s, specifically the dark, dramatic films featuring actor Lon Chaney, who often played grotesque, deformed, or mutilated characters in films like *Phantom of the Opera* (Julian, 1925) and *The Unknown* (Browning, 1927). Decades later, Chaney became known as the first horror film star, but when his films were released, he 'was known as a talented character actor who specialized in weird parts' because horror did not exist as a recognizable film genre in the 1920s (Benshoff 2014: 218). At that time, horror film was in its '*experimental* stage, during which its conventions are isolated and established' (Schatz 1981: 37 italics in the original).

These films were not made with the specific intention of attracting youth audiences, nor did they feature youths in prominent roles. Shary notes, 'A tradition of movies related to the supernatural goes back to the earliest days of cinema, although rarely did these films address teenagers' (2014: 187). After *Caligari*, Expressionist cinema in Germany continued to explore the fantastic, with the most celebrated of these films being the poetic vampire tale *Nosferatu* (Murnau, 1922) and *Metropolis* (Lang, 1927), a dystopian fable. These films examined adult issues like unhappy marriages and dehumanization in a mechanized society. In the US, the 'new morality' of the Jazz Age emphasized 'cynicism' and 'sexual license' (Cook 2016: 134), and dark melodramas featuring Chaney, often playing twisted and deformed characters, reflected the traumatic aftermath of World War I (Skal 1993: 65–68). There was a 'general dearth of films about adolescence' (Shary

2005: 7). Whenever young people appeared in these films, the characters 'were designed to exploit adult fears about youth rather than appeal to real youth audiences' (6).

This trend continued in 1931 with the birth of the Classical horror film. Genres enter their '*classic* stage' when their 'conventions reach their "equilibrium" and are mutually understood by artist and audience' (Schatz 1981: 37). Universal scored at the box office with *Dracula* (Browning, 1931) and *Frankenstein* (Whale, 1931) while Paramount's release of *Dr. Jekyll and Mr. Hyde* (Mamoulian, 1931) received critical praise and won a Best Actor Oscar for Frederic March as the titular split personality. These films solidified horror cinema's style, conventions, and themes. As the US was in the depths of the Great Depression and expendable money was scarce, Hollywood's strategy was to appeal to the broadest audience possible. The vertically integrated Hollywood studio system was firmly established by the 1930s, mass-producing films to play in theaters they owned in downtown urban areas. During this time, 'Film studios did not feel compelled to make products aimed at children, who generally had no income for entertainment, and who could be assumed to enjoy the same films their parents enjoyed' (Shary 2005: 5).

Universal helped keep the habit of movie-going afloat during the Great Depression by making horror movies that appealed to the whole family. As one of the minor studios, Universal did not own a 'chain of downtown first-run theaters and was forced to concentrate its production and distribution efforts on subsequent-run houses in suburban and rural areas' (Cook 2016: 190), making it imperative for them to produce films for the whole family. The studio's horror films were its biggest hits of the decade, and newspapers gave accounts of entire families attending *Frankenstein* (Browning 2014: 232), with adults too riveted to notice their children were terrified. Universal's first wave of horror films lasted from 1931 to 1936, when Joseph Breen, head of the Production Code Administration (PCA), began to so strictly enforce the Code that making horror films was nearly impossible.[3]

Horror was not dormant for long, however, and it was during the second wave of Universal's horror films that the sleeping giant of youth horror began to awake. In 1938, an internal review of the PCA conducted by Francis C. Harmon, the PCA's chief vice president, found that Breen had overextended his authority, and 'Breen's position was comparatively weakened' (Vasey 1997: 223). Around the same time, a nation-wide double-bill re-release of *Dracula* and *Frankenstein* netted Universal half a million dollars (Weaver et al. 2007: 183). With Breen's strict approach now perceived as a liability that would hamper big box office from horror films (Bernard 2014: 43), it was not surprising that the Code was loosened. This relaxed regulation likely inspired Universal to begin production on *Son of Frankenstein*

(Lee, 1939), their third Frankenstein film. *Son* does not have the low-key, moody, and Expressionistic atmospherics of Universal's previous horror films. This time around, the mad scientist (Basil Rathbone) has a curly-haired toddler son, Peter (Donnie Dunagan), who offers cute comic relief. Peter is one of very few preadolescents featured in 1930s horror cinema.

Son was indicative of the direction Universal would take with horror during the 1940s. Rick Worland explains that while '*Frankenstein* et al. had been pitched to adults, the sequels were increasingly aimed at juvenile audiences' (2007: 69). The difference between the 1930s version of *The Mummy* (Freund, 1932) and 1940s *The Mummy's Hand* (Cabanne, 1940) offers an example. The first film tells a story of exotic danger, as the resurrected Imhotep (Boris Karloff) seeks to win the love of an Egyptian woman (Zita Johann) whom he believes is his resurrected lover. *The Mummy's Hand* is a proto-Indiana Jones tale about a group of adventurous archeologists on an expedition to Egypt running afoul of an evil cult in control of a mindless mummy, a story 'tailor-made for the action house trade' (Weaver et al. 2007: 229). Films of this type were similar to action serials from Poverty Row studios being produced at the same time for 'children and juveniles for Saturday matinee shows' (Tzioumakis 2017: 69). While there is a 'perceived aesthetic decline of the horror in the 1940s' (Worland 2007: 71), it would be a mistake to write off all 1940s horror as juvenile fare, as the decade did produce several sophisticated horror films.[4] However, Universal's 'kiddie-oriented fright flick[s]' like *Frankenstein Meets the Wolf Man* (Neill, 1943), *House of Frankenstein* (Kenton, 1944), and *House of Dracula* (Kenton, 1945) demonstrated that youth horror had gained a toehold in the film industry (Weaver et al. 2007: 509).

1950s: Birth of Youth Horror

The 1950s was a transformative decade for the film industry that saw a huge shift in audience demographics. After a peak year in 1946, movie attendance began dropping dramatically and would continue to do so until the early 1970s (Cook 2016: 334–335). However, one demographic began attending the movies in droves: teenagers. As the post-World War II economy strengthened in the early 1950s, Americans began leaving the city and moving to the suburbs, where affordable houses were plenty. Living outside the cities, many homeowners now had to commute to work, so car sales skyrocketed, leading to the prevalence of car culture. During this time, 'Teenagers began buying (or at least driving) cars' and tended to meet up with other friends in cars and 'congregate around a single hangout' (Shary 2005: 17). One of the most prominent hangouts for teens in the 1950s was the drive-in movie theater, an exhibition venue that exploded in popularity between 1946 and 1953 when 2,976 drive-in theaters opened in the US (Davis 2012: 36). The drive-in offered teens a dark space to engage in a variety of activities, and the running time of the films—most drive-ins offered double bills—gave teens a good excuse for being gone for three or four hours. The youth market became the most significant audience for the movies in the 1950s, eventually making up 52.6 percent of movie-goers (39).

When young people became the dominant movie-going demographic, major studios attempted to tap into this audience through the production of several science fiction films. The genre had proven itself to be the 'preferred fantasy form' of young audiences in the early 1950s (Doherty 2002: 117). Thomas Doherty argues that sci-fi films of this era possessed a potent subtext: fear of the hydrogen bomb. With the first H-Bomb being tested on 1 November 1952, atomic dread was the 'essential subject' of sci-fi teenpics (*ibid.*). Major studios turned to sci-fi in hopes of securing profits during uncertain times as the film industry underwent significant reconfiguration. The Supreme Court's ruling in *United States v. Paramount, et al.* in 1948 stripped the vertically integrated Hollywood studios of their theaters, making it prudent for major studios, since they no longer had guaranteed theatrical prospects, to roll back production and '[focus] on maximizing profits through fewer and costlier releases' (Heffernan 2004: 5). Another method of increasing revenues was the implementation of 3-D technology, which paired well with sci-fi's emphasis on special effects. John Carpenter cites Universal's *It Came from Outer Space* (Arnold, 1953), one of the films from this cycle, as sparking his interest in filmmaking (Anchor Bay 2013a).

Unfortunately for the majors, their attempt to tap into the youth audience had mixed results. The majors still employed the Depression-era strategy of appealing to 'a crossover audience of adults, adolescents, and kids' (Doherty 2002: 115). Warner Bros.' creepy *House of Wax* (De Toth, 1953) would interest youth audiences, but the film's 3-D effects demanded that patrons dish out extra money for a ticket, which may have been a turn-off for youth audiences with less disposable income. It became clear by the mid-1950s that the major studios, with crossover films meant for both young people and adults, were not equipped to cater to the needs of an ever-increasing youth audience. In 1956, an article in *Variety* diagnosed that 'the major studios were not doing enough' to reach youth audiences (Davis 2012: 39), a conclusion seemingly corroborated that year when MGM's *Forbidden Planet*, 'a Freudian extraterrestrial update of *The Tempest* labeled "Space Patrol" for adults' (Doherty 2002: 118), performed below studio expectations.

It could be that the majors were not willing to get as bizarre, shocking, and outrageous enough for young people, as teen audiences demonstrated a preference for 'weirdies,' a name trade papers gave to films for youth audiences that could be classified as horror, science fiction, or a strange hybrid of both (119). At this time, a slew of independent producers and their 'weirdies' stormed the youth film marketplace. One of these independents was AIP, a company that owed a great deal of its success to '[taking] teenage subculture on its own terms' (132). The horror teenpics produced by AIP and other independents often displayed a 'deliberate alienation of the older audience' in the ways they 'began to stretch the permissible limits of violence and gore' (Heffernan 2004: 68). This testing of the boundaries was enabled by the Supreme Court decision in *Joseph Burstyn v. Wilson, Commissioner of New York* (also known as '*The Miracle* Case') in 1952, which extended First Amendment protections to movies for the first time (Draper 1999: 187).

By the mid-1950s, weirdies dominated the teenpic box office, with 1957 being a banner year for youth horror. *The Curse of Frankenstein* (Fisher, 1957), produced in the UK by Hammer Films and distributed in the US by Warner Bros., was a radical retelling of the story of Frankenstein and his creation—played respectively by Peter Cushing and Christopher Lee, future horror icons—making Dr. Frankenstein 'ruthless, sadistic, and odiously suave' and loading the film with a generous amount of blood and gore (Heffernan 2004: 49). Shot on a $270,000 budget, the film was a hit for Warner Bros. in the US, grossing around $2 million by the end of 1957 (Doherty 2002: 115). Along with AIP's *I Was a Teenage Werewolf* (Fowler, 1957), *Curse* opened the floodgates for youth horror, with 52 horror films produced in 1957 and 75 in 1958 (122). With teens accounting for over half the movie-going population, movies featuring monsters who embodied feelings of 'psychological dislocation and social estrangement' with which teens '[felt] a kinship' ruled the box office (119). Among independents and companies from outside the US, Hammer continued to acknowledge this kinship with films like *The Brides of Dracula* (Fisher, 1960) which depicted vampirism as 'a troublesome youth cult' threatening to '[upend] the world of adult morality' (Williamson 2005: 79).

As horror teenpics took over the box office, horror took over the home via television. Studios realized television offered a potentially lucrative revenue stream. Since television networks needed content to fill airtime, studios began leasing feature films from their archives. In 1957, Universal, the king of monster movies in the studio era, leased 550 pre-1948 titles to Screen Gems, the television arm of Columbia Pictures, for $20 million (Heffernan 2004: 156). Screen Gems assembled 52 of Universal's horror films and sold them to affiliates in a package titled 'Shock Pictures.' Television markets across the US aired these 'Shock' films around Halloween of 1957 and created a ratings bonanza (Doherty 2002: 121), inspiring other distributors to lease their horror catalogs for broadcast. Screen Gems followed up with a 'Son of Shock' package (Heffernan 2004: 156). Dracula and the Frankenstein monster were remediated as kiddie icons in the late 1950s. According to Allan Fromme, an author of parenting books popular in the 1950s and 1960s, television made horror films safe for children; he assured children that horror movies on TV will only 'provide a smile with your milk and cookies at bedtime' (Doherty 2002: 121). Also making horror feel safer were a bevy of horror hosts, like Ghoulardi in Cleveland and Vampira in Los Angeles, who would introduce the films and pop in during the commercials with jokes. The year after the 'Shock' films debuted on television, Warren Publishing released the first issue of *Famous Monsters of Filmland*, a magazine edited by fantasy film memorabilia collector Forrest J. Ackerman, known affectionately as 'Uncle Forry' to his youthful readers, one of which was young John Carpenter (Boulenger 2001: 65). At the end of the 1950s, youth horror was in full bloom, with magazines like *Famous Monsters* on newsstands, a cavalcade of horror films on television, and movies by foreign producers like Hammer and US independents like AIP and William Castle, who made a sensation with his gimmick-riddled spookhouse films like *House on Haunted Hill* (1959), populating theaters and drive-ins.

1960s: Youth Horror Grows Up

Like youth horror, Alfred Hitchcock ruled at the box office, with star-studded blockbusters like *Rear Window* (1954) and *To Catch a Thief* (1955), and on television, with his hit series *Alfred Hitchcock Presents*, which debuted in 1955. Four years later, Hitchcock brought film and television together, producing a feature film that would be shot quickly and cheaply with a television crew. The director drew from the fertile terrain of youth horror. He purchased the rights to Robert Bloch's best-selling 1959 novel *Psycho*, which was based on the crimes of Ed Gein, a murderer and necrophiliac whose crimes stunned the world earlier that decade. The adaptation veered in a youth-oriented direction, as Gein-inspired killer Norman Bates was transformed from a balding, overweight middle-aged man to a good-looking young man (Anthony Perkins). Rolled out with 'a sophisticated ad campaign, a high-dollar version of the teasing come-ons beloved by AIP and William Castle' (Worland 2007: 86), *Psycho* was a smash at the box office. Although critics were initially reluctant to embrace the film (Jancovich 1996: 220), *Psycho*'s critical reputation grew over several years. Wood cites *Psycho* as a turning point in American horror cinema, when the monster was no longer foreign and supernatural, but rather was 'American and familial' (1979a: 19). Scholars like Clover would eventually declare *Psycho* 'the immediate ancestor of the slasher film' (2015: 74). Though Norman Bates prefigures the human monsters of the teen slasher, there is no direct line from *Psycho* to *Halloween* because Hitchcock's film did not kick off a string of similar slashers with killers stalking teenage victims (Nowell 2011: 58). Hitchcock's film did inspire a handful of adult-oriented thrillers like *The Innocents* (Clayton, 1961), *Whatever Happened to Baby Jane?* (Aldrich, 1962), and *The Haunting* (Wise, 1963) from the majors. Films that featured evil children like *The Bad Seed* (LeRoy, 1956), which predated *Psycho*, and *Village of the Damned* (Rilla, 1960) were from an adult point of view, reflecting parental anxiety over 'what their children might become' (Paul 1994: 277). Even William Castle, the king of gimmicky kiddie horror, directed several features in the 1960s that were more adult-oriented knock-offs of *Psycho*. For the most part, however, 'major Hollywood studios remained aloof from horror' for much of the 1960s (Worland 2007: 90).

Filling this void, independently produced horror teenpics grew more sophisticated, psychological, and brutal. Andrew Tudor claims that the 1960s is when horror cinema began to explore the 'fear of ourselves and of the ill-understood and the dangerous forces that lurk within us' (Tudor 1989: 217). The career of industrious teenpic director Roger Corman reflects this transition. Working fast and cheap, Corman directed over 20 films between 1955 and 1959. In 1960, AIP wanted to differentiate its films from other low-budget teenpics. Knowing Corman could get the most out of a marginal increase in money and time, they tapped him to adapt an Edgar Allan Poe short story from the public domain into a color film in CinemaScope. The result was *House of Usher* starring Vincent Price, whose salary made up a third of the budget (Gray 2004: 72). AIP was nervous that the film did not feature a monster, but Corman assured them that the family's house was the monster (71), a sign that Corman aimed to explore internal, not external struggles. The film was a hit, leading to a series of Corman-directed Poe films for AIP, during which Corman's technique evolved as he used 'overt symbolism, stylized color, and flashback narrative structure' to explore inner mindscapes (Heffernan 2004: 112). Horror teenpics also became more violent. AIP scored another hit when they handled US distribution for the Italian-made *Black Sunday* (Bava, 1960), a film that begins with a spike-filled mask being hammered onto the face of a young witch played by Barbara Steele, who quickly became an international star.[5] *Black Sunday*'s director, Mario Bava, would later follow up with *Blood and Black Lace* (1963), the story of a masked killer picking off fashion models in grotesque ways. Even more graphic were the ultra-low-budget films of director Herschell Gordon Lewis, who ushered in the era of the gore film with *Blood Feast* (1963), which featured a cannibalistic Egyptian caterer (Mal Arnold) dismembering bodies in vividly graphic ways. About a year later, the Supreme Court's decision in *Jacobellis v. Ohio* (1964) offered protections for theater owners from protests or threats from local authorities (Lewis 2000: 129), giving exhibitors license to screen films with graphic content that could not be aired on television.

1968 was a key year for youth horror with the release of *Night of the Living Dead*, directed by George A. Romero, and *Rosemary's Baby*, directed by Roman Polanski. The films encapsulate the spectrum of youth horror of the upcoming decade. Shot in rural Pennsylvania on a shoestring budget, *Night* tells the story of a small group of survivors trapped in a farmhouse by flesh-eating zombies. Romero explores horror's capacity for sociological allegory as he makes the group metaphorical of the United States tearing itself apart during a time of social upheaval due to various tremors of countercultural revolt. In crafting his allegory, Romero utilized the extreme gore of films like *Blood Feast* featuring shots of zombies devouring human flesh that allegedly horrified a theater full of children when it screened at a matinee show in Chicago (Heffernan 2004: 213). Less rough around the edges than *Night* was *Rosemary's Baby*, which tells the story of a woman (Mia Farrow) who is impregnated with the spawn of Satan. Hutchings argues that horror cinema histories often deemphasize *Rosemary's Baby* because its 'high production values' strip it of the 'authenticity and social engagement' of a film like *Night* (2014a: 49). However, the film's big-budget status as a Paramount production is one reason it is significant. With the film industry in deep recession, studios pursued projects with cross-promotional possibilities, such as a tie-in with a book, play, or television show (Cook 2000: 27). *Rosemary's Baby* was an adaptation of Ira Levin's best-selling novel, giving it a 'pre-sold' element (Hutchings 2014a: 51). The film's marketing was sleek and tasteful. The poster featured the austere image of a baby carriage in profile on a mountaintop against a green sky. Behind, a blow-up of Mia Farrow's profile lies horizontally, faintly appearing through the mist. The film's marketing prefigures the 'high concept' approach that would grow more prominent in Hollywood. The ideal high concept film can 'be sold in a single sentence and [has] potential to be marketed through stars and merchandising tie-ins' (Wyatt 1994: 7–8). High concept is 'the look, the hook, and the book. The look of the images, the marketing hooks, and the reduced narratives' (22). The advertising of *Rosemary's Baby*, when paired with its clear hook (Satan has a child) and novel tie-in, employs the high concept approach. *Rosemary's Baby* may differ from the low-budget *Night*, but the films share one crucial element: they both feature a monstrous child—compare the birth of Satan's child to the preteen girl (Kyra Schon) in *Night* who, when resurrected, kills and eats her parents—that ruptures the status quo. The power of both sides of the horror film spectrum is filtered through images of vicious youths.

1970s: Ratings and Revisions

Two changes significantly altered the 1970s youth horror film market. One was the introduction of the ratings system created by the Motion Picture Association of America (MPAA). The system introduced an R rating that limited the viewership to those above 17 years old and allowed more violence and nudity. The MPAA ostensibly adopted this system to help parents determine which films were appropriate for children. Ideally, the ratings system could help avoid the type of the confusion theater owners experienced when booking *Night of the Living Dead* for an afternoon matinee (Heffernan 2004: 213), making sure certain films with mature content are clearly marked for exhibitors and parents. However, MPAA-member studios were less concerned with 'protecting children' and more concerned with using the ratings system to control 'participation in the marketplace' (Lewis 2000: 150). The system enabled the major studios to offer a 'wide[r] range of product lines' (151), immediately latching onto 'sensationalist material they had previously left to independents like AIP' (Maltby 2003: 179). As long as a major studio film kept sensationalistic material within certain parameters, it could obtain an R rating ensuring its easy circulation through the theatrical marketplace (Lewis 2000: 151).

The ratings system was an efficient mode of industry self-regulation, wherein the studios set their own intentionally vague standards for what constituted an R rating. This system cleared the way for successes like Warner Bros.' horror blockbuster *The Exorcist* (Friedkin, 1973), a demonic-possession movie with graphic content. The ratings system also allowed MPAA-member studios 'to ghettoize independently produced and distributed films' by branding any film with violence and/or nudity that MPAA members deemed excessive with an X rating, which would severely limit the number of theaters that would screen the film (Lewis 2000: 173). Such was the case with *Last House on the Left* (Craven, 1972), the brutal story of parents taking revenge on the criminals who raped and murdered their daughter. Sean Cunningham, the film's producer, and Wes Craven, the director, fought with the MPAA but could not come to an agreement on an R rated cut, as the MPAA had little investment in the success or failure of a low-budget independent (171).

Regardless, Craven's film still 'performed well on the exploitation circuit' (Nowell 2011: 122), showing that there was room for occasional success in the ghetto of the American film market. For example, *The Texas Chain Saw Massacre*, a low-budget independent, ended up being 'one of the twenty highest grossing films' of 1974 (Cook 2007: 132). One of the most-often noted features of the film is its lack of gore, despite the title's sensationalistic come-on. Hoping for a rating that would allow young audiences to see the film, director Tobe Hooper consulted with the MPAA for advice on how to best edit violent sequences to receive a PG rating (Worland 2007: 298n). While he did not get the PG rating, the success of Hooper's film suggests that a low-budget horror film that played by the rules of the MPAA-member studios in terms of graphic content could be a hit. Accordingly, independent producers in the mid-1970s began shifting away from extreme violence and nudity in hopes of capturing larger audiences (Nowell 2011: 96).

The second change in the industry occurred when shifting gender dynamics led to the revision of 'the Peter Pan Syndrome,' which, in turn, led to the production of *Black Christmas*, the first teen slasher. Coined by AIP bosses Sam Arkoff and James Nicholson during the rise of the weirdie, the formula hypothesizes that studios will attract their 'greatest audience' by 'zero[ing] in on the 19-year-old male' (Doherty 2002: 128). While Arkoff and Nicholson were right to focus on youth audiences—in 1968, 16–24-year-olds made up 48 percent of film audiences (Nowell 2011: 64)—they did not anticipate how important the female contingent of the youth film market would be. *Love Story* (Hiller, 1970) and *The Way We Were* (Pollack, 1973) were two of the biggest hits of the early 1970s, encouraging production companies—especially independents—to specifically 'secure the patronage of young women' who flocked to these films (70–71). With these changes in mind, when Canadian filmmakers convened in 1974 in hopes of breaking into the American market, they 'combined the distinguishing elements' of four recent American hits: *The Exorcist, American Graffiti* (Lucas, 1973), *The Way We Were*, and *Magnum Force* (Post, 1973) (66). *The Exorcist* influenced them to make a horror film and populate it with teenage character types seen in *American Graffiti*. A turbulent romance was lifted from *The Way We Were*, and the gang of vigilantes in *Magnum Force* inspired the villain, an unseen killer. All these elements added up to *Black Christmas*, a film about a psychopath hiding in the attic of a college sorority house and picking off victims during the Christmas holiday. Despite the synthesis of these elements, *Black Christmas* was not a hit. The film's 1974 Canadian release showed promise, but in the US, the film fared poorly when released by Warner Bros. during the Christmas season (76). The film's modest success in Canada convinced Warner to give it another try with a platform release in the summer of 1975. Again, the film's box office faltered, and Warner withdrew it from circulation before the Christmas holiday (77).

Even though it was not a hit, *Black Christmas* provided a template for *Halloween* that Yablans, Carpenter, and Hill would follow, but only after making some changes to the type of female characters their film would feature. These revisions were informed by successful youth films released after *Black Christmas*. One change was in the demographics of the victim group, switching out the 'careerist university students' of *Black Christmas* with 'small-town teenage girls' (84). Nowell argues that two films encouraged this change. One was *The Pom Pom Girls* (Ruben, 1976), a low-budget film about a group of small-town high schoolers enjoying some summertime fun. *The Pom Pom Girls* was produced and released by the independent studio Crown International. In overseeing the production of the film, Crown International production executive Marilyn Tenser had an approach that ran counter to AIP's Peter Pan Syndrome, claiming that female youths 'influence our box office' and 'are the ones that decide what movie a couple is going to see' (qtd. in Nowell 2011: 86). Tenser's philosophy paid off as *The Pom Pom Girls* performed well at the box office, garnering $4.3 million in rentals, a sizeable figure for a small independent like Crown (Nowell 2011: 87). The second film that, according to Nowell, influenced *Halloween*'s focus on female teenagers in a small-town high school setting was *Carrie* (De Palma, 1976), an adaptation of Stephen King's novel about a shy, telekinetic girl (Sissy Spacek) driven to murder by the bullying of her cruel classmates. An independent production distributed by United Artists, *Carrie* garnered big box office dollars, rave critical reviews, and Oscar-nominations for its two female leads, Spacek and Piper Laurie (91). Taken together, the success of *The Pom Pom Girls* and *Carrie* was a testament to the profitability of teen films that featured 'small-town female protagonists in film-types that were thought to be male-oriented' like the teen comedy and the horror film (89).

Following revisions to the Peter Pan Syndrome, the conceptualization of *Halloween* began by foregrounding its female characters. Yablans's original title for the film—'The Babysitter Murders'—suggests the film's female-centric approach. Since the development of the female main characters was deemed 'so important to *Halloween*'s commercial prospects' (83), Hill wrote the dialogue for Laurie, Annie, and Lynda, the idea being that a female writer would achieve a ring of feminine authenticity and produce compelling female characters. To this end, Hill carefully crafted three archetypal teenage girls: the brainy (Laurie), the brash (Annie), and the beautiful (Lynda) (see Figure 1.2). *Halloween* inarguably emphasizes the female teenage perspective over the male. Laurie, Annie, and Lynda are much more developed as characters than their counterparts. Lynda's boyfriend Bob, the only male character in the victim group, is by far the least developed of the film's teen characters.

Figure 1.2 Brainy, brash, and beautiful: The girls of *Halloween*

Photo courtesy of Kim Gottlieb-Walker, www.Lenswoman, 'On Set with John Carpenter'

Halloween: A Synthesis of Youth Horror

While the film plays to current trends in youth horror by courting the cov-
eted female demographic, it also builds upon youth horror's past. The idea
of setting the film on Halloween affords the film endless opportunities to

explore connections between the holiday and youth culture, a relationship with a darker dimension than Bob Clark could conjure between Christmas and youth in *Black Christmas*. Halloween myths often find youths in danger of abuse from adults—for instance, urban legends of adults handing out candy with razors hidden inside; other times, youths are the ones posing a threat toward adults or other children during the carnivalesque holiday.[6] Most relevant to this discussion of youth and the Halloween holiday, however, is the unique relationship between the holiday and entertainment media. The Halloween holiday 'supports, and is supported by, a big chunk of the entertainment industry. . . . Its rituals are more those of media audiences than those of communities interrogating their cohesiveness and hospitality' (Mathijs 2009). This is the case in the film, as Laurie, Tommy, and Lindsey structure their Halloween night around Doctor Dementia's movie marathon, while Haddonfield's streets are mostly silent with very little communal activity. *Halloween*'s depiction of the connection between Halloween and media rituals opens a portal to youth horror's past, revealing some surprising connections between Carpenter's film and the weirdies of the drive-in era.

Doctor Dementia's broadcast of *The Thing from Another World* and *Forbidden Planet* points to a number of subtle sci-fi elements in *Halloween* that demonstrate its familial connection to the weirdies. This kinship is evident in Michael Myers, *Halloween*'s masked madman, who appears to be a new model of sci-fi's killer robot. Michael's blank white face mask makes him look artificial, like a mannequin whose flesh color has not been painted on. As he glides in and out of the shadows, Michael's movements are unnervingly mechanical in their precision. Leeder observes that there is 'something *robotic* about Michael' and notes that Carpenter's vision of Michael was inspired by the deadly robotic gunslinger played by Yul Brynner in *Westworld* (Crichton, 1973), a sci-fi thriller about killer robots run amuck in a futuristic theme park (2014: 52). Accentuating Michael's robotic nature is Carpenter's electronic score, which often accompanies his movements (55n). For instance, when Michael attempts to strangle a nurse (Nancy Stevens) during his escape from custody at Smith's Grove Sanitarium, his actions are intensified by a sting from Carpenter's score that sounds like steam shooting out of the exhaust pipe of a futuristic machine. As the nurse nervously waits in the driver's seat of the station wagon that has come to transport Michael to court to stand trial as an adult, Michael jumps onto the roof. She rolls down the window, and Michael's arm, synchronized with Carpenter's electronic hiss, shoots into the window like a piston and grabs her throat. Later, when a seemingly-dead Michael lying on the floor mechanically sits up and turns his head to lock Laurie in his sights, the movement is emphasized by a single ominous note of Carpenter's score.[7] When Tommy sees Michael carrying Annie's dead body into the Wallace residence, spaceship noises from *Forbidden Planet* emanate from the television, creating an auditory metonymic chain connecting Michael and sci-fi (*ibid.*). Michael also transubstantiates atomic dread of the 1950s-era weirdies. Earlier in his career, Carpenter dipped into the realm of weirdie sci-fi with his first feature-length film, *Dark Star* (1974), a pitch-black comedy about a spaceship carrying an atomic bomb that gains sentience with grave consequences.[8] Wood argues that 'the unkillable and ultimately inexplicable monsters' of the slasher film whose 'mysterious and terrible destructive force we can neither destroy, nor communicate with, nor understand' embody the 'nuclear anxiety' of the Cold War that continued from the 1950s into the 1980s (1986: 168). References to *The Thing from Another World* and *Forbidden Planet* make this connection more explicit in *Halloween* than it is in any other slasher film.

Halloween's connections to youth horror of the drive-in era are more obvious but no less rich. If *Halloween*'s sci-fi elements are embodied by Michael, many of its horror tropes are present in Michael's nemesis, Dr. Loomis. By casting Donald Pleasence as Loomis, Carpenter taps into the Gothic atmosphere of Hammer pictures. The Hammer connection is clear in the actors Carpenter initially hoped to cast. His first choice was Peter Cushing, a Hammer icon who portrayed Victor Frankenstein and Professor Van Helsing, among others for the studio. When Cushing turned down the role, Carpenter turned to Christopher Lee, another Hammer icon who was known for his portrayals of the Frankenstein monster, Count Dracula, and others. After Lee rejected the role, Carpenter's third choice was Donald Pleasence, perhaps best known as James Bond arch-villain Blofeld. The casting of Pleasence was crucial to the production, as evidenced by his $20,000 salary out of the film's $320,000 budget (Anchor Bay 2013b).[9] He was the film's most seasoned, well-known actor. Pleasence's English accent and 'old world' presence call back not only to Hammer horror, but also Corman's Poe adaptations with Vincent Price.

In keeping with the Gothic atmosphere of Corman's Poe movies, Pleasence's most memorable and iconic scene in *Halloween* takes place when Loomis and Sheriff Brackett venture into the dilapidated Myers house on Halloween night. Standing in the darkness, Loomis tells Brackett about his first encounter with Michael. The Myers house is one of the first of the slasher film's 'Terrible Places,' a location cursed by past trauma. The 'Terrible Place' of the slasher film is an update of the ruined castles of Gothic literature like the one seen in Horace Walpole's novel *The Castle of Otranto*, first published in 1794, which, like the Myers house, is haunted by incestuous trauma.[10] As Carpenter generously lays on the atmosphere, the Myers house becomes a suburban stand-in for a castle from a Hammer film, one of Corman's AIP Poe pictures, or a William Castle spook show. As a moody descending four-note phrase from Carpenter's score plays, Loomis recalls:

> I met this six-year-old child with this blank, pale, emotionless face and the blackest eyes . . . the devil's eyes. I spent eight years trying to reach him and then another seven trying to keep him locked up because I realized what was living behind that boy's eyes was purely and simply evil.
>
> (see Figure 1.3)

Long-time *Fangoria* magazine editor Tony Timpone cites the 'camp factor' added by Pleasence's performance as one of *Halloween*'s most appealing aspects (Anchor Bay 2013b), suggesting Loomis is a descendant of the 'campy' and 'hammy' mad scientists of youth cinema's past (Mathijs and Sexton 2011: 82–83). Several slashers that followed *Halloween* feature a veteran actor from Hollywood's past that lends them a patina of respectability (Betsy Palmer in *Friday the 13th*, Ben Johnson in *Terror Train*, Farley Granger in *The Prowler* [Zito, 1981]), but none of these veteran actors recall youth horror's past like Pleasence's Loomis, especially considering the relationship between Loomis and Michael.

Doppelgangers have populated horror since its literary roots, but the dichotomy between scientific creator and monstrous creation represented by Loomis/Michael in *Halloween* has its antecedents in two key films in youth horror history. One is *Curse of Frankenstein*. As the ostensible 'hero' of the film, Loomis may seem far from Cushing's ruthless portrayal of Victor Frankenstein, but there is a certain malevolence to Loomis—he

Figure 1.3 Loomis in the spookhouse

acknowledges that he must appear to be 'a very sinister doctor'—that suggests Loomis's 'treatment' of Michael is partially to blame for Michael's behavior. *Halloween*'s other antecedent is AIP's hit weirdie, *I Was a Teenage Werewolf*. In this film, Tony (Michael Landon), an alienated teenager, goes to 'headshrinker' Dr. Carver (Whit Bissell) looking for a way to control his anger. Carver has a well-intended but insane goal to send the human race 'to its early beginnings' and inadvertently transforms Tony into a werewolf. The parallels with *Halloween* are clear. Before visiting Carver, Tony is not necessarily evil; bullying from his peers makes him aggressive. Michael's murder of his sister is certainly more horrifying than Tony's bursts of rage, but when Michael's father unmasks him after the murder, he does not look maniacal but confused, as if he has no comprehension of what he has done. Ultimately, both Tony and Michael submit to the care of psychologists and emerge more monstrous than before. Regardless of whether Loomis is to blame for Michael's condition, the thematic threads of untrustworthy science and misguided misfit monsters connect *Halloween* with the weirdies.

While *Halloween* draws from the 1950s era, it also demonstrates youth cinema's maturity in the 1960s and 1970s. As youth films go, *Halloween* often feels old and wizened. Contributing to this air of maturity is the film's references to *Psycho*, a film that attempted to '[confer] respectability on the horror film' and '[attract] audiences who would never have gone to see a Hammer film' (Marriott and Newman 2010: 100). Leeder argues that *Halloween* 'clearly [exalts] Hitchcock's masterpiece as an ur-text' (2014: 10), drawing from the film's twisted psychology in its depiction of a child from an antiseptic suburban environment turned murderer. The influence of other dark youth horror films released after *Psycho* are pronounced in *Halloween*, ranging from the somber ghosts of *The Innocents*, which inspired the disquieting images of Michael silently staring at Laurie as he stalks her (Zinoman 2011: 182), to the paranoiac panoramas and bombastic scores of Italian horror films like *Deep Red* (Argento, 1975) and *Suspiria* (Argento, 1977) (Anchor Bay 2013a; '*Halloween*' 1990: 36).

One component of the darker youth horror that did not carry over to *Halloween*, however, was gore. Danny Peary describes *Halloween* as a synthesis of Hitchcock, Val Lewton, William Castle, and the 'graphic violence' of post-*Night of the Living Dead* horror (1981: 123). The last entry on Peary's list is baffling as the film contains little graphic violence and no gore. Actually, in the years following *Halloween*'s release, critics praised the film for its restraint (Nowell 2011: 96). Additionally, Carpenter and Hill later claimed that the film's lack of blood was a conscious artistic decision. On a 1994 commentary track, Hill explains, 'We tried to do this with really good taste,' and Carpenter is satisfied that there is 'almost no onscreen,

Figure 1.4 Violence 'in really good taste': Annie's shadowy death

overt violence in the film' (quoted in Anchor Bay 2013a) (see Figure 1.4). However, Hill's and Carpenter's comments elide the economic concerns that informed the decision to downplay gore and violence, as Yablans and Akkad wanted to avoid trouble that films like *Last House on the Left* had when they clashed with the MPAA (Nowell 2011: 95). The independents were aware that the X rating would virtually eliminate any chance that the film would return a profit, and 'Yablans was part of the sea change sweeping the American independent sector' that favored content compatible with the ground established by the MPAA (Nowell 2011: 96). Playing by the rules paid off for *Halloween*. The film ended up being the tenth highest grossing film of 1978 and was the only independently distributed film in the top ten highest grossers that year.

The ratings system gave control of the marketplace to the major MPAA-member studios and distributors and was buttressed by Supreme Court decisions in anti-obscenity cases like *Miller v. California* (1973) which—*unlike Jacobellis v. Ohio*—made theatrical venues more vulnerable to local censorship and protest (Lewis 2000: 262–264). Decisions in the Paramount Decree, '*The Miracle* Case,' and *Jacobellis v. Ohio* set the stage for youth cinema: the first brought about its necessity from a business standpoint by opening up a vacuum in the market for youth films, the second assured freedom of expression and relaxed regulatory restrictions, and the third protected exhibitors. However, the re-entrenchment of the majors via their renewed control over content and exhibition overturned these decisions. As such, *Halloween* marked the end of an era for youth cinema, as its style and marketing campaign looked toward a new era that left the drive-in behind and headed toward the multiplex.

1980s: Blockbusters, High Concepts, and *Halloween*

The late 1970s was another time of immense change that had far-ranging implications for youth cinema. During the drive-in era, weirdies would often be released following a 'saturation' model; producers and distributors specializing in teenpics would release the picture to as many exhibition sites as they could. As such, these teenpics often had what the industry calls 'marketability,' but they often lacked 'playability' (Lewis 2003: 65). The Allied Artists release *Attack of the Crab Monsters* (Corman, 1957) provides an example. The hyperbolic title is wildly evocative and places it within the weirdie idiom, making the film marketable and guaranteeing a reliable turn-out during its opening weekend. But it is doubtful the film has much 'playability,' which refers to a film's ability to generate good 'word of mouth' that will attract more audiences for subsequent screenings. Most audiences interested in seeing *Attack of the Crab Monsters* would probably see it on its opening weekend, and the film's threadbare plot and bargain-basement production value are unlikely to inspire good word of mouth. However, the low-budget film likely turned a profit during its opening weekend, if only because of the wide release. During the 1950s and 1960s, major studios and prestige productions did not utilize the saturation model, relying instead on the platform release model, especially for films that seemed to have playability. This model slowly rolled out releases and steadily increased the number of screens for a film, the idea being that good word of mouth would slowly build an audience for the film.

This approach began to change in the early 1970s, when an industry reeling from an intense recession saw in the huge box office of films like *The Godfather* (Coppola, 1972) and *The Exorcist* a potentially lucrative model: the blockbuster.[11] A key characteristic of the blockbuster strategy is the aforementioned saturation release, a practice the majors borrowed from small independent distributors of teenpics and other low-budget films. While saturation booking was once 'a means of throwing a movie away' and getting the most out of a subpar product, the major studios began to use it as 'a way of signaling [a film's] importance' (Cook 2007: 134), and they had the money to give blockbusters releases on a previous unheard of scale. Universal's *Jaws* (Spielberg, 1975) is generally considered as the first blockbuster of 'the new Hollywood' era with a successful then-massive opening on 464 screens (Schatz 2003: 25).

Three years later, when the major studios were well into the blockbuster era, *Halloween* scored big, ironically, by employing the platform release strategy once used by the majors. Unable to strike a distribution deal with the majors, Yablans worked with regional exhibitors and secured *Halloween* a release in Kansas City and Chicago in late 1978 (Yablans 2012: 175–177). The film did great business in both cities. In Chicago, nationally syndicated reviewers Gene Siskel and Roger Ebert gave the film a rave review, encouraging Yablans to open the film in larger markets (*ibid*). Unlike many low-budget genre pictures that were given a saturation release in drive-ins, *Halloween* had 'playability.' Word of mouth was strong, and ticket sales steadily climbed until March 1979, when the film began getting attention in trade papers (Nowell 2011: 101–103). All the majors had passed on the film, but *Halloween*'s surprise success hinted that the film's concept could be adaptable to the blockbuster release strategy. As Nowell notes, *Halloween* was 'crafted to capitalize on developments in blockbuster filmmaking' and demonstrates solid 'commercial logic' by 'locating content' from other blockbuster films like *Jaws*, *The Omen* (Donner, 1976), and *Star Wars* (Lucas, 1977) and assembling it to craft Michael, a heavy-breathing, demonic, and unstoppable force signaled on the film's soundtrack by highly recognizable music (9 and 92–94). As soon as Compass announced a sequel, Hollywood power player Dino De Laurentiis contacted Yablans, offering to buy sequel rights for his company (Yablans 2012: 191). Taking on production of the film, De Laurentiis struck a distribution deal with Universal. By the time Universal handled the release of *Halloween II* (Rosenthal, 1981) on Halloween eve 1981, the blockbuster release was standard, and *Halloween* made a perfect transition into this era. The sequel opened in 1,211 theaters in the US and grossed $25.5 million ('Franchises: *Halloween*' n.d.). *Halloween*'s concept found itself at home during the blockbuster era.

Halloween also benefitted from its integration of high concept style and marketing—even more so than *Rosemary's Baby* had a decade ago—embodying the ethos of 'the look, the hook, and the book.' The high concept film is partly 'differentiated through the emphasis on style in production' (Wyatt 1994: 20). Carpenter described the film as 'a stylistic exercise' and crafted it in a polished, commercial style that disguised its low budget (Boulenger 2001: 97). Leeder observes that the film's 'stylistic flourishes'—its use of anamorphic widescreen to realize its environs, Panaglide/Steadicam to give the feeling of floating paranoia, and Carpenter's relentless electronic score to keep the audience on edge—are all 'smoothly integrated' (2014:11). The film's style gives it 'the look' so important to high concept. *Halloween*'s style was deftly sold by its marketing, which did an excellent job selling 'the hook.' Understanding the challenges of independently distributing the film in a tough marketplace, Yablans 'spent a lot of time working on the key art' for the film's advertising (2012: 174). Its marketing parlayed the film's most commercial elements into an advertising campaign, epitomizing 'the integration of the film with its marketing,' essential for high concept films (Wyatt 1994: 20).

The most appealing aspects of the film inform its iconic poster. As Nowell explains, the poster's tasteful use of 'near-monochromatic images' resembled posters for other major studio horror releases that had done well at the box office, and the combination of an upraised hand wielding a knife combined with the jack-o-lantern promised 'mild horror in the context of a fun experience' (2011: 100). The film's tag line 'The Night *He* Came Home!' takes the film's already simple story and simplifies it further, creating the perfect 'hook.' The poster is topped off by the film's logo. The most potent and marketable high concept can be sold through a short title effectively made into an instantly identifiable logo (Wyatt 1994: 4). Yablans's idea to title the film *Halloween* and set it during the holiday pays off in dividends here. The single word title gives the film a stately, austere quality that is complemented by the use of ITC Serif Gothic typeface, which '[combines] gothic simplicity with traditional roman elegance' ('ITC Serif Gothic' n.d.). The Halloween-orange outlining the white words make for an instantly recognizable logo. The film became a blockbuster hit on the back of a marketing campaign that was able to embody all aspects of high concept: the look, the hook, and, eventually, the book, especially as the film's simple narrative quickly inspired a novelization of the film in 1979.

Halloween foreshadowed nearly all the elements it would take for a youth horror film to be successful in the blockbuster era. Many histories of youth horror argue that *Halloween* 'truly inaugurated' the slasher cycle (Shary 2014: 8), but the cycle was over by 1981. Perhaps more significant is how *Halloween* offers an example of crafting a youth horror brand name. The blockbuster era began around the same time as the rise of the shopping mall (Schatz 2003: 26), and these two developments dovetailed significantly, especially in regard to youth audiences. As Shary explains,

> With the relocation of most movie theaters into or near shopping malls in the 1980s, the need to cater to the young audiences who frequented those malls became apparent to Hollywood, and those audiences formed the first generation of multiplex moviegoers.
>
> (2014: 7)

As movies appeared more often alongside other consumer goods in mall multiplexes, blockbuster films were expected to establish a brand name that could act as 'the spearhead for numerous concurrent revenue streams' and 'prove sufficiently popular to inaugurate a "franchise"—a series of sequels whose shelf life could extend for decades' (Cook 2007: 134). This development makes it necessary to approach films of the multiplex blockbuster era as both 'text and commodity, intertext and product line' (Meehan 1991: 62).

The importance of establishing a brand name—even for a low-budget slasher movie—is demonstrated by the success of another low-budget slasher, *Friday the 13th*. Unlike *Halloween*, *Friday the 13th* was picked up by a major MPAA-member studio for distribution when Paramount gave the film a saturation release that grossed over $16 million before the end of 1980. Sean Cunningham, *Friday the 13th*'s producer and director, first provoked interest in the film with the title alone; in July 1979, he posted a full-page advertisement for the film in *Variety*, promising it would be 'The Most Terrifying Film Ever Made!' (Bracke 2006: 17). Thus, the journey of *Friday the 13th* begins with the promise of an exploitable title, and after Cunningham independently produced the film, Paramount was able to turn the film into a smash success by creating a marketing campaign that made the most of the title. Paramount's marketing created a recognizable logo for the film by using scratchy, blood-red letters. The logo was less elegant than *Halloween*'s, a difference that reflected the film's content, which was a bit gorier than Carpenter's film. At the same time, however, Paramount's use of 'comic-book style' design on the film's poster assured audiences that the content would not be too extreme, so as to not scare off any potential multiplex audiences (Nowell 2011: 140–141). Like Compass before them, Paramount successfully crafted a teenpic brand name.

This brand name would hold the studio in good stead during the onslaught of teen slasher films that poured into the box office in the months following *Friday the 13th*'s successful release. *Prom Night*, a Canadian-made production starring Jamie Lee Curtis, performed well, but follow-ups *Terror Train* and *My Bloody Valentine* (Mihalka, 1981) failed to score. Things got worse as the market was inundated with slasher films throughout 1981, and interest in the slasher film waned (Nowell 2011: 230–231). Out of a group of seven slasher films released between February and September 1981, only one was a success: Paramount's *Friday the 13th Part 2* (Miner, 1981), which did at least double the business of all the other films during this period (Nowell 2011: 233). Nowell observes that the marketing for *Friday the 13th Part 2* emphasized its connection to the first film, from the trailer to the poster, which consisted of only the film's title—written in the same rough and jagged type face of the original—against a black background. Nowell notes that the poster's tagline, which reads 'The body count continues . . .' stresses continuity with the first film (236). The marketing of other slasher film releases from 1981 also attempted to attach their films to *Friday the 13th*, but to little avail, suggesting that the brand name was most important in securing business during the multiplex era.

The attempt to suggest continuity of a successful brand is present in the marketing materials for *Halloween II*, released in October 1981, months after dismal returns of other slasher films. Like the poster for *Friday the 13th Part 2*, the *Halloween II* poster goes to great lengths to emphasize its connection to the previous film. Most of the elements of the original poster have returned; the monochromatic color scheme, the pumpkin, and the logo are all present. This time, a skull emerges out of the pumpkin, and there is no hand wielding a knife, a choice that may reflect the diminishing returns of slasher fatigue in the theatrical market. Continuity with the first film is most important, even down to the tag line: 'From The People Who Brought You "HALLOWEEN" . . . More Of The Night *He* Came Home.' In fact, the poster may have adhered to the brand name a little too closely, as the words 'ALL NEW' appear at an angle on the side of the poster, as if the distributor worried that it might be so similar that it looks like an ad for a rerelease of the original film. For the most part, the rest of the decade would prove that franchising a recognizable brand name was crucial for success in the youth horror market. There would not be another successful brand name established in youth horror until 1984 with New Line's *A Nightmare on Elm Street* (Craven, 1984) which featured a concept—a murderer stalks and kills you in your dreams—and visual hooks—a razor-fingered glove among them—that fit perfectly with the tenants of high concept marketing. The multiplex mentality held strong.

Conclusion

This chapter argues that *Halloween*, by stringing together many of the reoccurring obsessions of youth horror cinema, compiles an index of youth horror's past. Youth horror exploded onto the film market in the early 1950s after the fallout of the Paramount Decree. The majors attempted to appeal to youth audiences with pictures like *House of Wax* and horror/science fiction hybrids like *It Came from Outer Space*, the latter of which reflected society's atomic dread in the wake of the first hydrogen bomb test. However, the major studios were not as well-positioned to appeal to youth audiences as the independents were, which they did with aplomb, pioneering the 'weirdies,' bizarre films that blended horror and science fiction. Throughout the 1950s, weirdies projected a youthful ethos by mirroring teenage frustration with their portrayal of monsters as troubled, alienated outsiders distrustful of the establishment and authority. The distrust grew deeper in the 1960s, as youth horror plumbed the depths of human depravity and explored a culture grown paranoid due to distrust of others and the self. All the while, horror cultivated a following among teens and preadolescents in a domestic setting as horror films from decades past were remediated on television. With Doctor Dementia's televised Halloween horror movie marathon, *Halloween* kept open a portal to the past while also taking on many of the changes in the youth horror market during the late 1960s and early 1970s like increasing attempts to appeal to female viewers. *Halloween*'s creators also profitably embraced blockbuster filmmaking and high concept marketing, both of which would play significant roles in youth horror cinema during the multiplex era.

This chapter maintains that ultimately, *Halloween*'s significance may not be bound up in its status as the first or most influential slasher film, but rather as a compendium of youth horror's past and a bellwether of its future. Youth horror had been captivating audiences for several decades, but as it was making the transition from the drive-in to the multiplex, the subgenre started to gain attention from another, perhaps unlikely, audience: academia.

Notes

1 *The Thing* consistently tops many, if not all, online 'best of' listicles and fan polls of Carpenter's films. IMDb's *Through the Lens* episode about the 'Carpenteresque' describes *The Thing* as 'a filmic landmark, almost the definition of the word Carpenteresque' ('Defining Carpenteresque' 2018). In a 2013 interview, Carpenter noted that *The Thing* is the film he is most asked about (Carpenter 2013).

2 Nowell's history of the first slasher cycle covers 1974 to 1981 (2011). The first cycle peaked commercially in 1981, but slasher films continued to be released throughout 1982 and 1983.

3 For more about industry self-regulation during this era, see Black (1994); Doherty (1999).

4 See Jancovich (2014).

5 The next year, AIP would pair Steele with Price for Corman's second Poe adaptation, *The Pit and the Pendulum* (1961).

6 See Leeder (2014: 60–69).

7 Actor/stuntman James Jude Courtney quotes this movement/moment in his performance as Michael in 2018's *Halloween* (Green, 2018), a testament to the iconic status of Nick Castle's performance.

8 Carpenter would return to sci-fi with his remake of *The Thing* and his films *Starman* (1984), and *Ghosts of Mars* (2001).

9 This figure is taken from Joseph Wolf in Anchor Bay (2013b).

10 The theme of incest is discussed in more detail in Chapter 2.

11 See Cook (2000) for more about the recession of the late 1960s and early 1970s.

2   Familial and Societal Failure

Reading Youth and Ideology
in *Halloween*

As noted in the previous chapter, youth horror cinema was booming in the 1970s, with films populating both the mainstream and the margins of the cinematic marketplace. A number of notable horror films from this era featured youths as main characters or were geared to appeal to youth audiences or both. *Deathdream* (Clark, 1972) features a young soldier returning home from the Vietnam War as a blood-thirsty zombie.[1] A duo of teenage women fall prey to a violent gang in *The Last House on the Left*. A young man is demonically possessed in *The Possession of Joel Delaney* (Hussein, 1972), and a pubescent girl is possessed by a demon in *The Exorcist*. A woman gives birth to a monstrous baby in *It's Alive* (Cohen, 1974). A shark devours teens and pre-teens in *Jaws*. In *Carrie*, a high schooler uses her telekinetic powers to slaughter her bullies. Following in the youth horror tradition, *Halloween* told the story of teenagers stalked by a masked assailant. With youths accounting for almost half of box office revenues, youth horror ruled at the drive-in and multiplex.

Horror movies also began attracting attention from another, more mature audience: academics. Although film studies appeared sporadically at the university level at various points before the 1960s,[2] it officially entered the curriculum in the late 1960s. Infused with radical, countercultural politics of the time, much of film studies adapted already-existing disciplines like anthropology, semiology, and psychology to undertake an ideological analysis of film that considered how Hollywood films not only reinforce but also question or subvert dominant ideology. Film studies soon turned its attention to horror cinema. In 1979, a group of Canadian academics including Andrew Britton, Richard Lippe, Tony Williams, and Robin Wood, employing critical approaches drawn from a re-interpretation of the works of Marx and Freud, published a collection of academic essays about horror cinema titled *The American Nightmare*. While several films were praised for their subversion of social institutions, *Halloween* took a drubbing, with Wood citing Carpenter's film as the end of an era of ideologically rich horror films from the 1970s that attacked dominant ideology and as the beginning of an era of conservative horror in the 1980s that reinforced dominant ideology (1986: 189–197). Wood's methodology 'left its mark on subsequent horror criticism' and made it 'commonplace for horror films to be labeled as politically progressive or reactionary' (Hutchings 2014b: 298), and *Halloween* and Carpenter's other films were labeled as reactionary (Grant 2004: 15).

Nevertheless, *Halloween* shares with politically progressive horror of the 1970s a disdain for the authorities and institutions put in place by dominant ideology, retaining many of the contradictions and complexities of 1970s cinema. Roughly a decade after the publication of *The American Nightmare*, Andrew Tudor constructed another framework for analyzing horror cinema (1989: 211–224). While Wood's model focused on how horror films represent the bourgeois heteronormative family and its attempts to mold 'ideal' inhabitants for patriarchal capitalism, Tudor moved away from the microcosm of the family to the macrocosm of society, its institutions, and the ability or disability of these institutions to protect its inhabitants (1989: 217). Tudor's taxonomy produces a reading of *Halloween* that finds the film more critical of dominant ideology.

This chapter argues that Tudor's framework ultimately draws out a more nuanced analysis of *Halloween*'s depiction of youth. Wood reads the film as politically reactionary partly because of the ways it portrays youth. He feels that Michael is presented as a monstrous 'Other' and that the film, to its detriment, neglects to analyze the social forces that shaped Michael. Further, he believes the film depicts teenagers as hedonistic revelers deserving of punishment from a puritanical slasher. However, Tudor's taxonomy foregrounds how institutional failure in the film—the failure of community, education, law, and science—affects Haddonfield's youth. Drawing from Tudor's paradigm, this chapter contends that, from an ideological perspective, *Halloween* is best understood as a mediation on how social institutions fail young people and leave them to fend for themselves, a scenario at the heart of many teen slasher films.

The American Nightmare: Academia and Horror Film

Film studies as an academic discipline emerged in the mid-to-late 1960s, bringing with it much of the countercultural politics of the time (Maltby 2003: 527). Scholars embraced insights from Black Power movements; adopted Marxism's focus on class, power, and ideology; and reverse-engineered frameworks for studying gender and sexuality from Freud, crafting a methodology focused on the triad of race, class, gender. Ideological analysis was also a 'motivating force behind . . . psychoanalytic and feminist film theory in the 1970s' (533). With its focus on gender and sexuality, the application of psychoanalytic theory was meant to be a 'politically sensitive activity that could contribute to a transformation of wider social relations' (535). Psychoanalytic theory sought to dismantle the power of dominant ideology embedded in Hollywood cinema. Film studies took root in the academy during a moment when it seemed that the monolithic institutions of capitalism and patriarchy were briefly on the ropes from the pummeling they had taken by the counterculture.

Wood and his compatriots felt studying horror cinema offered an opportunity to unveil the cruelty of capitalist patriarchy, revealing these institutions as inimical to the humane advancement of civilization. According to Wood, the horror film dramatizes society's struggle to oppress all those who differ from 'normal' (straight, white, male) and to repress 'abnormal' impulses within itself. Wood argues that US horror in the 1970s was fueled by 'the whole pervasive sense of ideological crisis and imminent collapse' of social institutions during the decade (1986: 121). This was a 'a historically specific crisis in American society' brought about by 'concerns over the Vietnam War and the protests against it, the Watergate scandal, the civil rights movement, feminism [and] discomfort with . . . dominant social structures and belief systems' (Hutchings 2014b: 297). In 1979, Wood and Richard Lippe organized a horror film retrospective to take place during the Toronto International Film Festival. The retrospective included film screenings, seminars, and the publication of a booklet titled *The American Nightmare*.

In the booklet, Wood outlines horror film's basic formula: normality is threatened by the monster. In the Classical Hollywood horror film, normality consists of capitalist patriarchy and the accompanying social institutions that perpetuate it. Conversely, the monster represents all those who are oppressed by normality and/or embody normality's repressed impulses and energies. The relationship between normality and the monster, for Wood, 'constitutes the essential subject of the horror film' (1979a: 14). Many horror films depict normality as fulfilling for all its inhabitants, and the monster as an inhuman, alien threat that must be defeated by social institutions. Thus, the narrative does not acknowledge the connection between normality and the monster, that the monster is 'normality's shadow' (*ibid.*), an entity made up of normality's repressed energies and desires. Wood acknowledges that his formula does not easily apply to all horror films and notes that 'as a general rule, the less easy the application, the more complex and interesting the film' (1979b: 59). In these 'more complex' horror films, the relationship between normality and the monster is not as clear cut but instead is more ambiguous. These films, Wood believes, have radical potential. The narrative of these films erodes the barriers between normality and the monstrous, leading the audience to feel ambivalent about normality and the monster. Normality seems more constrictive, and the monster grows more sympathetic. Wood argues that this sympathy felt for the monster 'extends to our attitude to normality' (1979a: 15), leading one to question those institutions that uphold normality.

According to Wood, the 1970s saw a proliferation of horror films that reflected the lack of confidence in American institutions in the wake of the counterculture movement, Vietnam protests, and the Watergate scandal. He argues that how a horror film represents the monster's struggle against normality reveals the film's underlying political position. To rate a horror film's political stance, Wood uses a metric that ranges from 'progressive' to 'reactionary.' Films that display an ambivalence toward normality, depict the monster as having a motive related to its oppression/repression, and reveal the often-hidden connection between normality and the monster are labeled 'progressive.' These films, according to Wood, demonstrate the untenability of patriarchal capitalism, stress the necessity of revolution, and suggest the creation of a society governed by a more equitable ideology. Prominent among Wood's 'progressive' horror films are Romero's *Night of the Living Dead*, his follow-up *Dawn of the Dead* (1978), and films directed by Larry Cohen such as *It's Alive* and *God Told Me To* (1976). He finds *The Texas Chain Saw Massacre* 'essentially nihilistic' but nevertheless admirable as it depicts the annihilation of a world corrupted by patriarchal capitalism (1979a: 19–22).

Falling on the other end of Wood's spectrum are those he feels either attempt to recuperate capitalist patriarchy and/or lament its disintegration. He designates these films 'reactionary.' One film he labels reactionary is *The Omen*, which he believes performs the same apocalyptic function as *The Texas Chain Saw Massacre* with a key difference: *The Omen* pines for the 'bourgeois capitalist patriarchal Establishment' even as Damien the devil-child brings about its destruction (1979a: 19). The final part of Wood's essay, titled 'The Reactionary Wing,' discusses films that Wood feels are politically regressive in their attitudes. These films do not depict the monster as normality's shadow; instead, the monster is 'non-human' and has no discernable motive, suggesting that normality is innocent of any wrongdoing in its enforcement of surplus repression (1979a: 23). Thus, these films uphold the necessity of normality and its defense, even if it may be a fruitless effort. Prominent among Wood's reactionary wing are David Cronenberg's early films—*Shivers* (1975) and *Rabid* (1977)—which he feels depict sexuality as loathsome and destructive to bourgeois society (1979a: 24). Another film Wood labels reactionary is *Alien* (Scott, 1979), in which 'sexuality [is] so rigorously repressed' that it 'returns grotesquely and terrifyingly in its monster' (1979a: 27). Cronenberg's films and *Alien* share an often-repulsive body horror that Wood feels extends to the film's wider attitudes toward sexuality and dominant ideology.

Halloween as 'Reactionary' Horror

Sandwiched between Wood's critique of Cronenberg and his dismissal of *Alien* is a passage about *Halloween*. Even though Wood places it in the same reactionary drawer, his initial attitude toward the film is more measured than his critique of Cronenberg. Wood does not wish to place *Halloween* in the same bracket as Cronenberg's films, noting that 'Carpenter's films reveal. . . an engaging artistic personality . . . a delight in skill and craftmanship, [and] a pleasure in play with the medium' (1979a: 24). Wood finds Carpenter's 'film buff charm' and intertextual references to past films 'cunning' even if a little confused (24). Carpenter says that Wood even once sent him a copy of one of his essays (Leeder 2014: 32), which indicates that Wood had at least some affinity with Carpenter's work. Or maybe Wood felt it would do Carpenter some good to read his essays. Throughout the early 1980s, his opinion of the director soured. Wood initially did not wish to group Carpenter with Cronenberg, feeling that Carpenter is the more engaging creative persona. A few years later, however, Wood's position changes considerably. In a 1983 essay, Wood amends his preference of Carpenter over Cronenberg, dismissing Carpenter because he 'lacks precisely that "artistic authenticity"' that Wood acknowledges in Cronenberg's work, even if he does not admire it (1983: 128). Carpenter quickly fell out of favor with Wood, and his valuation of *Halloween* seems to decline further during the following years.

This decline is on display on Wood's 1986 book *Hollywood from Vietnam to Reagan*, which contains a revised version of his essay from *The American Nightmare*. For the book, Wood extracted much of 'The Reactionary Wing' from the original essay and moved it to a separate chapter titled 'Horror in the 80s.' For Wood, horror cinema in the 1980s follows the lead of films by Spielberg and Lucas, what Wood's compatriot Andrew Britton calls 'Reaganite Entertainment' (Britton 2009: 99). These films construct the audience as children and reassure them that after the social and political upheaval of the 1960s and 1970s, things have been restored back to how they should be: social institutions have stabilized, the patriarchal family is reunited, and traditional values have been reinstated. Films from the Spielberg/Lucas camp assure audiences that rebellion and revolution are unnecessary because the world is as it should be. Reactionary horror in the 1980s performs this same function. Any monstrous disruption can be contained by returning things back to 'normal.' As Britton explains, Reaganite entertainment frames any progressive social change as impossible (101). Thus, in Reaganite horror, if a return to normality is not enough to contain the threat, no other solutions are possible, so it is best to just let things fall apart because 'there's nothing you can do, anyway' (Wood 1986: 168). In an introduction to the 'Horror in the 80s' chapter, Wood calls *Halloween* a 'divisive film' that marks the point where the progressive horror of the 1970s ends and the reactionary 1980s begin (1986: 193), further emphasizing the point by removing the material about Cronenberg that originally opened 'The Reactionary Wing' section and moving *Halloween* to the forefront as an exemplar of reactionary horror.

Two main components of *Halloween* that make it 'reactionary' have to do with the film's representation of youth: 1) the depiction of the child as monstrous 'Other' via young Michael Myers and 2) the depiction of teenagers who are killed by Michael during their sexual escapades. Wood's reading of *Halloween* highlights how youth plays an important part in his framework; Shary notes that Wood's scholarship is 'integral to the imaging of youth' in horror cinema (2014: 170). Wood argues that the source of horror in American cinema is the release of surplus repression—often referred to as 'the Return of the Repressed'—with this liberation conceived as monstrous (1979a: 7–8). According to Wood, those things most repressed in our society are sexuality, bisexuality, female sexuality, and sexuality of children, with childhood sexuality being the most 'fundamentally' repressed (1979a: 9). He describes the prohibitions placed upon childhood sexuality as a 'process moving . . . from *re*pression to *op*pression' (9).

Given the degree to which oppression from the bourgeois adult world forces children to repress their sexuality, it is little surprise that children appear on Wood's list of 'Other' figures that often emerge as monstrous in the horror film. Wood defines the 'Other' as 'that which bourgeois ideology cannot recognize or accept but must deal with . . . in one of two ways: either by rejection and if possible annihilating it, or by rendering it safe and assimilating it' (9). The 'Others' on Wood's list are those oppressed —women, racial and ethnic minorities, the proletariat—that are made to embody normality's repressed impulses and are often punished for them. Wood singles out children as perhaps 'the most oppressed section of the population' (10), arguing that 'the "otherness" of children . . . is that which is repressed within ourselves, its expression therefore hated in others: what the previous generation repressed in us, and what we, in turn, repress in our children' (*ibid.*). Thus, the child as monstrous Other is a personification of adult anxiety that children will do what adults secretly long to do: break out of the shackles of oppression and release all their repressed energies.

Before *Halloween*'s monstrous child Michael, the intensity of the image of the child as Other would simmer under the surface in horror cinema up until the late 1960s when it would explode during the 1970s and after. Earlier, the child as monstrous Other appeared in such films as *The Bad Seed*, *Village of the Damned*, and its sequel *Children of the Damned* (Leader, 1964). However, these films disavow the possibility that these monstrous children are normality's shadow and that their Otherness is born out of the normative adult world's repression and oppression. Instead, these monstrous children are the result of defective genetics or alien intervention. In *The Bad Seed*, suburban housewife Christine Penmark (Nancy Kelly) discovers that her daughter Rhonda (Patty McCormack), a seemingly-perfect 8-year-old, is a psychopathic murderer. The possibility that bad parenting led to Rhonda's condition horrifies Christine, but the film later reveals that Christine was adopted and her birth mother was a serial killer, suggesting that Rhonda inherited murderous genes from her grandmother. The mysterious incidents leading to the birth of a throng of malevolent telekinetic children in *Village of the Damned* and *Children of the Damned* are never fully revealed, but the films hint that an alien invasion-via-impregnation may be the culprit. Similarly, *Night of the Living Dead* intimates that radiation from a returning space probe caused the zombie outbreak that results in a little girl rising from the dead to murder and consume her parents.

When monstrous children became ubiquitous in the 1970s, their motives become clearer and more directly related to their parents and the social/ political milieu, making films of this nature more progressive by Wood's metric. However, the child-as-monster does not immediately appear in films that Wood and company would consider progressive. 1973's *The Exorcist* depicts one of the most recognizable cinematic child monsters with Reagan (Linda Blair), a demonically possessed 13-year-old girl. However, Wood's compatriot Andrew Britton denounces the film as one of the worst offenders of the reactionary wing, a film that represents the release of repression via Reagan's possession as repulsive and demands its punishment in order to reinstate dominant ideology.[3] Other films in the demonic-child cycle, like *The Omen*, do not fare much better by Wood's estimation. Conversely, Larry Cohen's *It's Alive* and sequel *It Lives Again* (1978) strike Wood as the most ideologically progressive. The first film tells the story of an expectant married couple (John P. Ryan and Sharon Farrell) who give birth to a monstrous killer baby. A pharmaceutical company executive (Robert Emhardt) fears that the baby is a side effect of birth control pills produced by his company and seeks to have the baby destroyed before his company can be found liable. However, an exact reason for the baby's deformed state and super strength is never revealed, as it is also hinted that environmental pollution may have caused the abnormal birth.

The non-specificity of the baby's origins and the depiction of the family that produced the baby lead Wood to believe that Cohen's baby monster symbolizes 'disturbance about heterosexual relations, male/female gender roles, the family, the contemporary development of capitalism, its abuse of technology, its indifference to the pollution of the environment, its crass materialism, callousness, and greed' (1986: 102). In *It's Alive*, the monster is created by normality and reflects its monstrousness, a theme developed further in *It Lives Again*. Wood argues, 'Cohen's films never repress the possibility of imagining that the world might be changed; indeed they implicitly encourage it' (1979c: 80), making them the very definition of progressive horror. At the conclusion of his essay on Cohen in 1979's *The American Nightmare*, Wood compares *It's Alive* to *Halloween*. Even though he has not yet entirely soured on Carpenter, he claims that *Halloween* 'does nothing new' while Cohen 'extends the boundaries of the genre . . . to the point where the horror movie becomes impossible and must logically give way to some form of revolutionary movie' (1979c: 86). Placing *Halloween* in opposition to the progressive *It's Alive* foreshadows the prominent position *Halloween* would eventually hold in Wood's canon of reactionary horror. At the middle of these crossroads between progressive and reactionary stands the image of the youth as Other, with Cohen's baby looking forward and Carpenter's child looking backward.

Michael, *Halloween*'s child-as-monster, ends up being a reactionary figure for Wood due to how the film disavows the possibility that bourgeois ideology created this child monster, even though the opening suggests it (see Figure 2.1). After the film's opening credits, title cards establish the setting as 'Haddonfield, Illinois' on 'Halloween Night 1963.' Then, the audiences sees from young Michael's perspective as he approaches the family home and spies on his sister and her boyfriend (David Kyle) through the living room window as they make out and eventually go upstairs. He then slips around to the back of the house, walks in the back door, takes a butcher knife from a kitchen drawer, waits until his sister's boyfriend leaves (presumably after a lightning round of sex), sneaks upstairs, dons a clown mask, and stabs his sister in the chest until she is dead. He then runs down the stairs and out of the front door. Just as Michael exits the house, his parents pull up in a

Figure 2.1 Michael Myers: Child as monstrous 'other'

car and get out. His father (George O'Hanlon Jr.) asks 'Michael?' and pulls off the mask. The camera cuts to a reverse angle and reveals the identity of the killer as a six-year-old boy in a clown suit. The shot tracks away and cranes up above the tableau of Michael holding a bloody knife bookended by his onlooking parents and then cuts to black.

Halloween's opening is rich with possible connotative meaning, beginning with the image of the house. David Roche explains that the setting immediately creates 'a synecdoche of white patriarchal middle-class suburban America' (2014: 44–45). The Myers family is established as 'unremarkable middle class WASPs' (Leeder 2014: 74). As Michael watches from outside the window, Judith and her boyfriend continue to make out on the living room couch, and the boyfriend jokes around by picking up a clown mask and pretending to kiss her through it. The couple heads upstairs. After the boyfriend leaves and Michael ascends the stairs with knife in hand, he spies the clown mask, now laying discarded on the floor, and puts it on. Paul argues that Judith's boyfriend wears the mask to hide 'their furtive sexual act . . . from others' (1994: 322). In the milieu that the film's opening has established, premarital sex would be discouraged. Michael dons the mask to hide a similar impulse, but his action takes the repression engendered by the social milieu to its logical conclusion: murder, an act of destruction, substituted for sex, which surplus repression relegates to procreation.

Paul's reading of the mask dovetails with Wood's theory that the monster represents a release of repression. In the case of *Halloween*, Wood views Michael as emblematic of the 'sexual repression of children' (1979a: 26). According to Wood, at play here is 'the incest taboo that denies sexual feeling precisely where the proximities of family life most encourage it' (*ibid.*). Although the film offers only a glimpse of the Myers house's layout, it appears to be a breeding ground for repressed desires to simmer under the surface before violently erupting. Michael's room sits opposite of Judith's, with no hallway or door between them. When Michael finds her, Judith is sitting topless in front of a vanity mirror, wearing only her underwear and lackadaisically brushing her hair. Given that Judith sits in the open doorframe separating her room from Michael's—she would be visible from Michael's bed—young Michael has likely seen her in this state in the past. Under bourgeois capitalist patriarchy, Michael's repressed emotions can manifest only as violence. Wood calls *Halloween*'s opening 'remarkable' and feels it sets up the film as possibly 'the definitive family horror film' with a 'child-monster' that is clearly 'product of the nuclear family and small-town environment' (*ibid*).

However, according to Wood, the remainder of the film does not follow through on the promise of its opening minutes. The first scene concludes with a crane shot that ascends into the air and hovers over the frozen tableau of Michael and his shocked parents. Robert C. Cumbow observes, 'The crane shot up and away, dwarfing the characters in the context of their surroundings, is a shot . . . most commonly used as an end title shot' (2000: 51). The film's abrupt cut to black reinforces a sense of finality, and in some ways, it is a conclusion, as the opening seems somewhat disconnected from the rest of the film. As Steve Neale notes, the film never again returns to a shot from Michael's POV; even though a great deal of the film finds Michael spying on his prey, none of these shots are from his subjective, first-person perspective (2004: 361). Michael's parents never appear again, suggesting that *Halloween* may not be the 'definitive family horror film' since it does not explore the intricacies of the family that produced the child-monster. Wood argues that the rest of the film disavows the possibility that Michael's monstrosity could be a product of bourgeois patriarchal repression. Contrary to what the film's opening may suggest, Michael is not positioned as 'normality's shadow' or the result of bourgeois repression. Instead, he is something completely alien, unrelated to normality's machinations. As Sheldon Hall puts it, Michael 'is from Haddonfield but not of it' (2004:71). Richard T. Jameson describes Michael as 'cosmic-evil' typical of *The Omen* era (2009). Similarly, Murray Leeder argues that Michael represents a threat akin to otherworldly Lovecraftian monsters (Leeder 2014: 87–93). Dr. Loomis constantly insists that Michael be treated as a being of pure evil and tells Sheriff Brackett that, as a child, Michael had 'the blackest eyes . . . the devil's eyes.' For Wood, Loomis's description of Michael places *Halloween* in the cycle of Satanic horror films like *The Exorcist* and *The Omen*, which he classifies as reactionary.

From this perspective, *Halloween*'s downbeat ending reads as one typical of Reaganite horror. *Halloween* fits comfortably among certain American films from the later 1970s like *All the President's Men* (Pakula, 1976) and *Rocky* (Avildsen, 1976) that emerged from what Wood calls 'a huge sigh of ideological relief' after the disruptions of the counterculture had been quelled, a feeling that presaged attitudes of the Reagan era (1986: 162). Wood describes Loomis as 'the most extreme instance of Hollywood's perversion of psychoanalysis into an instrument of repression' (1979a: 26), but even if he is an 'instrument of repression,' he is still unable to contain the upheaval caused by Michael. Loomis empties his revolver into Michael at the film's conclusion, but Michael survives and disappears into the night. The film concludes with a sequence of shots of all the domestic spaces Michael has terrorized during the course of the film, all the way from the Doyle household to the dilapidated Myers house. Layered over these shots is the sound of Michael's heavy breathing, insinuating that no place in the cozy, small-town bourgeois environment is untainted by his presence. Repression has failed, and since no other possible explanation is offered for Michael's actions besides him being totally evil, there are no other lines of defense. Reaganite horror depicts the social conditions of the world as immutable. Thus, *Halloween* cannot conceive of an alternate realm outside of the patriarchal bourgeois world that has been obliterated by a monster for which it refuses to take any responsibility.

Beyond its representation of the child-monster, *Halloween* may also be read as reactionary because of how it depicts teenagers, another example of how the representation of youth figures prominently in Wood's schema for reading horror cinema. Stereotypical depictions of horny teenagers being picked off in their pursuit of sex and/or drugs and alcohol are now commonplace, a widely recognized trope of slasher cinema. Before this stereotype became ubiquitous, *Halloween*'s release precipitated some of the early discussions of the possible implications of these conventional teenage characters. In his review of the film, Jonathan Rosenbaum makes a connection between teenage transgression and death, especially when it comes to the film's female characters. Rosenbaum writes that *Halloween* belongs to a 'popular puritanical genre' he calls the 'Mainstream Simulated Snuff Movie' or MSSM (1979). In these films, 'suspense is generated by an audience waiting for a woman to be torn apart by a maniac, and the act is "morally" prepared for—unconsciously sanctioned—by identifying her with illicit sex' (1979). Thus, female sexuality is punished by violent death in *Halloween*. Wood agrees with Rosenbaum: 'The killer's victims are all sexually promiscuous, the one survivor a virgin; the monster becomes . . . simply the instrument of Puritan vengeance and repression rather than the embodiment of what Puritanism repressed' (1979a: 26). A cursory look at the film seems to bear out this reading: Judith is murdered after a tryst with her boyfriend, Annie is killed in the car when she is getting ready to pick up her boyfriend; Bob and Lynda are both dispatched after having sex; and virginal Laurie is the only teenage survivor.

By this rationale, *Halloween* inaugurated a series of slasher films that viciously eschewed the progressive politics of 1970s horror and redefined the image of the 'typical' youth in horror. The misogyny of slasher films was long taken as a given. Both Wood and Clover contend that, while both male and female youths are slaughtered, women are specifically punished for their femininity in these films (Wood 1986: 195; Clover 2015: 83). Further, Wood argues that slashers represent a 'disturbing inversion' of his formula. In Classical horror, normality is founded upon sexual repression, with the monster representing a release of this repression. However, the roles are reversed in slashers: normality is characterized by sexual permissiveness, represented by the horny teenagers who populate the films, and the monster, 'while still produced by repression, has essentially become a superego figure, avenging itself on liberated female sexuality or the sexual freedom of the young' (1986: 195). Wood feels that Classical horror films encourage, 'however ambiguously, an identification' between the viewer and the monster who seeks to disrupt repressive 'normal' society, an identification that feeds into the viewer's own subconscious desires to smash through society's boundaries. Conversely, slasher films encourage audiences to identify either with a monster that represents puritan vengeance upon a society grown too permissive or with victims who are punished for their transgressions, encouraging 'sexual guilt' among youth audiences (195, 196).

Scholarship often argued that *Halloween* was an example of how 'patriarchy positions women as subject to men (and their violence)' as it 'rehearses and restates that ideology as an assertion both of male aggression and male power and of male fear of women and female sexuality' (Neale 2004: 367). This is not to say that all scholarly assessments of *Halloween* denigrated the film as reactionary, misogynistic dreck. For instance, J. P. Telotte argues that, rather than encouraging the audience to revel in a world in which 'people are easily transformed into objects of voyeuristic attention, sexual pleasure, and finally homicidal mania' (1987: 127), *Halloween* invites the viewer to reflect on how these impulses are commonplace in Hollywood cinema. However, *Halloween* figures prominently in Clover's 1987 'Her Body, Himself.' Her theory of the pleasure male film audiences derive from slasher films is another symptom of misogynistic patriarchy and its (mis) use of women's bodies as explained by psychoanalytic film theory. Richard Maltby explains, 'By the early 1990s, "psychoanalytic film theory" and "contemporary film theory" had become more or less synonymous terms' (2003: 535), pointing out that psychoanalytic theory dominated film studies throughout the 1980s. If this was true about film studies in general, it was doubly true about horror film studies. Psychoanalytic film theory was not incredibly kind to slasher films or *Halloween*. If psychoanalytic discourses continued to dominate the study of horror cinema, *Halloween*'s position in the canon would be an uneasy one.

Halloween and Institutional Failure

A shift away from a strictly psychoanalytical perspective offers a more nuanced reading of *Halloween* and its depiction of youth. Wood finds the film's opening fascinating because of what it may reveal about Michael's psychological profile, but others are wary about delving into Michael's psyche as a way to interpret the film. Leeder warns that '"Profiling" Michael is a fool's errand' (2014: 20). Similarly, Paul argues there is no 'coherent motivation' much less a 'sexual motivation' for Michael's actions (1994: 321). Despite this, Paul speculates that Michael may be lashing out because he feels abandoned by Judith, who is supposed to be babysitting him but has thrown him over to spend time with her boyfriend (322–323). Mikel J. Koven also makes this point, suggesting Judith's 'poor babysitting' leads to her death (2008: 124). If one sees Judith as a person who has been instituted to protect a child from harming themselves or others, she has failed, allowing her brother to commit an atrocious act—and perhaps even leading him to commit it. Judith's failure to the institution of childcare foreshadows a series of institutions that will continually fail to protect young people.

Andrew Tudor offers a useful model for examining larger social structures and institutions in horror cinema. Mark Jancovich notes that Tudor's work moves beyond the 'reliance on various forms of psychoanalysis and their consequent emphasis on gender and the family' to consider horror cinema 'within a far broader social and historical context' (1996: 226). In Tudor's taxonomy, horror films generally fall into two categories: 'secure' and 'paranoid' (1989: 217). The secure horror film presents a world in which 'authorities [are] credible protectors of order' (*ibid.*). When faced with danger from an 'external "distant" threat,' authorities are able to use their 'effective expertise' to defeat the threat, leading to a 'closed' narrative with a clear resolution (*ibid.*). Since the expertise of authority is what defeats the threat, the secure horror film focuses on the experts. Conversely, the paranoid horror film features authorities who are not credible nor able to contain the disorder brought about by the threat, which is this time 'internal' and/or 'proximate' (*ibid.*). Since the authorities are ineffectual, the narrative lacks closure and remains open (*ibid.*). Also, paranoid horror focuses more on the victims who are left to fend for themselves in the absence of effective intervention from the authorities. Tudor argues that horror cinema slowly transitioned from secure into paranoid over the course of several decades and breaks down the history of the genre into three periods. The first period of horror cinema, lasting from the 1930s to the 1950s, was predominantly made up of secure horror. The second period, stretching from the late '50s to the early 1970s, was a time of transition between secure and paranoid when the genre was 'in a state of flux' (218). The final period, from the late 1970s onward, is dominated by paranoid horror.

Tudor reads *Halloween* as indicative of paranoid horror, claiming, 'At every turn, the world of *Halloween* . . . is thoroughly unreliable and insecure' (2002: 108), and many sources of paranoia in *Halloween* relate directly to the film's depiction of youth. One of the most significant of these is the paranoid horror brought about by the 'internal' source of horror in the film, which is Michael. Wood is frustrated because the film fails to develop the idea that the middle-class bourgeois family may be responsible for Michael and instead insists that Michael is pure evil, but Tudor's model encourages one to look beyond the family and consider larger social and institutional structures. Despite its innocuous suburban veneer, Haddonfield rarely feels like a safe place. As Sue Short describes it, Haddonfield is a place where 'everyone seems to know each other' but 'no one can be called upon in a time of crisis' (2007: 52). In his analysis of Carpenter's visual style, Sheldon Hall discusses how Carpenter uses formal elements to heighten suspense and anxiety throughout *Halloween*. He argues, '*Halloween*'s refusal to develop the psychology of its characters concentrates our attention on their role as components in a design or machine' (2004: 70). To this end, Carpenter's camera tracks his characters through a wide vista of small-town uncertainty and unease (70–75). Describing *Halloween*'s *mise-en-scène*, Jameson writes, 'Virtually every shot contains corners, apertures, fillable black holes fraught with ghastly potentiality' (Jameson 2009). As Jameson explains, Carpenter takes advantage of the anamorphic frame, staging elements in a panorama that makes 'unverbalizable' connections between characters and their surroundings (Jameson 2012). *Halloween* does not verbalize but nevertheless conveys through its visuals that Haddonfield is an uncomfortably open social space—a 'geography of horror' as Muir puts it (2000: 78)—in which children are often left to fend for themselves.

Unease is visually conveyed when Laurie first appears. A crane shot drifts to the left and slowly descends to reveal the Strode house. Laurie exits, textbooks in hand, presumably leaving for school. As she walks away, her father (Peter Griffith), a real estate agent, tells her to drop off a key at the Myers house. Laurie says she will remember as she walks down the sidewalk away from the camera, shrinking into the distance. As Laurie turns a corner, the film cuts to a far-away shot—somewhere between a long and extreme long shot—of Laurie crossing the street. From this shot length, Laurie is dwarfed by her surroundings: tall trees looming overhead, a wide street completely empty besides a few cars parked along the curb, everything eerily quiet as Carpenter's score plays nervously on the soundtrack. While the camera tracks with Laurie, she approaches a corner where Tommy runs toward her from deep in the frame along an intersecting sidewalk. This shot is the first extended look the film offers of present-day Haddonfield, and it sets a mood of agoraphobic dread for these youths. A parental figure, Laurie's father, appears briefly as Laurie leaves the house, but he does not offer much comfort or affirmation, as he orders her to perform a task for him. Youngsters are left to walk the streets alone.

Later, Laurie, Lynda, and Annie walk home from school along a street with overhanging trees that throw shadows on them, suggesting that even in the middle of the suburbs, danger looms ever-present (see Figure 2.2). The tall trees seem to cut them off from the rest of the neighborhood, which may be just as well since all of Haddonfield feels empty and ominous. When Michael drives in the station wagon he stole during his escape, his presence makes literal the danger that has already been intimated. As Paul explains,

Figure 2.2 The shadowy streets of Haddonfield

Halloween tells a story of 'terror in isolation' and the 'terror of suburban life' (1994: 323), and Carpenter uses stylistic elements to visually depict (to use Jameson's term) the 'unverbalizable' terror of children stranded in an empty world in a way that dialogue cannot. Wood denounces the film because he feels it attempts to disavow any suggestion that Michael is a product of his environment. But the way the film reveals the emptiness of Haddonfield's social world makes it easy to believe that it produced Michael, a killer bereft of emotion.

For young people, Haddonfield appears even bleaker when one considers the indifference of the town's institutions. Prominent among institutions that play a large role in the lives of youths is education. In youth films, the school is, as Shary describes it, 'a symbolic site of social evolution, with young people learning from and rebelling against their elders (and each other) in the ongoing cycle of generational adjustment and conflict' (2014: 29). Only three scenes in *Halloween* take place at school. Two of these scenes are at Haddonfield High, and the other unfolds at the intermediary school. Even though these scenes are brief, they reveal a great deal about the harsh world young people must navigate in Haddonfield.

The first high school scene finds Laurie in an English class. As the camera slowly tracks toward her sitting in a desk near the back of the room, the teacher (who is only heard, never seen) lectures about two authors, Costaine and Samuels,[4] and the different ways they write about the concept of fate. Laurie makes a note, absentmindedly glances out the window, and notices Michael, standing behind the station wagon and staring at her. Noticeably uncomfortable, Laurie meekly glances around as if to see if anyone else notices and looks out the window again, only to see Michael still there.

Perhaps because she suspects Laurie of daydreaming, the teacher asks Laurie a question. Taken off guard, Laurie asks, 'Ma'am?' The teacher, sounding somewhat irritated, demands, 'Answer the question.' Laurie offers a thoughtful response, and the teacher replies, 'That's right.' The teacher's approval is of little comfort for Laurie, however. She looks out the window again, and even though Michael is now gone, she is still uneasy and shakes her head, as if trying to fend off a feeling of dread. This is the first time Laurie sees Michael, and the teacher's failure to recognize the threat at this key moment foreshadows how adults in the film will remain largely oblivious to the danger facing the youth of their town.

The two other school scenes—one at the intermediary school and one at high school—are equally revealing. The scene in Laurie's classroom is immediately followed by a scene at Tommy's intermediary school that finds Tommy being bullied by three schoolmates. After they decide they have tormented him enough, they run away, and one of the boys runs into Michael, who has apparently been watching the incident from behind a chain-link fence. Michael lets the boy go and continues to follow Tommy from a distance as Tommy walks dejectedly away from school.[5] There are no authority figures around at Tommy's school to watch out for bullies or masked men stalking students as they walk home. These two school scenes—one with Laurie, one with Tommy—create the sense of a world where youths are in danger and adult authority figures are indifferent or entirely absent. A later scene—the third and final scene in an educational setting—succinctly captures the atmosphere of Haddonfield's educational system. At the end of the day at Haddonfield High, Laurie and Lynda begin their walk home by passing through a dark tunneled outdoor hallway. Their exit from school plays out in one shot that is approximately 30 seconds long. For the first half of the shot, Laurie and Lynda are enveloped in total darkness before they emerge. This shot subtly indicates that in Haddonfield, education is not a source of enlightenment; instead, it is one of those 'fillable black holes fraught with ghastly potentiality' that Jameson notices in Carpenter's *mise-en-scène*. In *Halloween*, education is an institution that does not recognize the threats that Haddonfield's young people face; rather, it turns a blind eye toward these perils, leaving its youths vulnerable to danger. When one considers the darkness at the heart of Haddonfield's institutions, it is not difficult to imagine how this environment produced Michael, a child with, as Loomis describes, 'the darkest eyes.'

Another notable hallmark of paranoid horror in *Halloween* is the failure of authorities as 'credible, protectors of order' (Tudor 1989: 217), as the film depicts the inability of law enforcement to stop Michael's killing spree. In *Halloween*, law enforcement is represented by Leigh Brackett, a character who plays a dual role in the story: he is Haddonfield's chief law enforcement officer and Annie's father. In terms of the narrative, Brackett is one of Carpenter's most deftly economical choices as he collapses the father figure into the representative of the law, thus allowing one character to represent two institutions—the family and the law—that fail the young people of Haddonfield. Several commentators have noted the absence of parents and parental figures in the film.[6] Reynold Humphries attempts to extrapolate theories for why Michael does what he does based on the little information the film offers about the Myers family (2002: 140). Similarly, one of the primary aspects bothering Wood about the film is its denial to explore the family as an institution that attempts to produce '"ideal" inhabitants' of heteronormative capitalist patriarchy but often produces neurotics (1979a: 26, 8). However, Carpenter's choice not to explore the Myers family as a normalizing institution that produced a monster in Michael, combined with his choice to make the most prominent father figure in the film a police officer, may signal that Carpenter is more interested in critiquing societal institutions and their unreliability than family dynamics and their impact on the young individual.

The untrustworthy nature of the police is underscored when Brackett first appears. As Laurie and Annie walk home from school, Laurie sees Michael peeking from behind a hedge. When Annie investigates, there is nothing there. Annie goes into her house, and as Laurie walks away, she keeps suspiciously glancing over her shoulder. She begins walking backward, afraid to turn away from the hedge for a second, and walks into Brackett, who suddenly appears behind her. Laurie lets out a yelp and profusely apologizes. Brackett assures her it is all right, but there is something subtly sinister when Brackett grins and says, 'You know, it's Halloween. I guess everyone's entitled to one good scare, huh?' The scene suggests that law enforcement may be as much of a threat to Haddonfield's young people as Michael is. As David Woods notes, many of Carpenter's films depict a struggle between 'ordinary citizens' and 'the forces which threaten them,' creating a 'divide between an "us" and a "them"' (2004: 22). Woods explains that the 'they' in Carpenter's films is often either a force 'identified with the supernatural' or 'an officially sanctioned authority' (*ibid.*). *Halloween* has both: Michael and the Haddonfield police.

Halloween's teenagers are placed in opposition to inept and corrupt social institutions throughout the film. In terms of societal structures, Barry Keith Grant argues that Carpenter's films resemble those of Howard Hawks, but with a key difference. As Grant explains, 'Hawks's characters may live briefly on an existential precipice, but the safety net of dominant ideology always is stretched underneath' (2004: 13). Grant offers Hawks's 1948 Western *Red River* as an example of this schema: 'Hawks's cowboys may be cut off from the law while on the cattle drive in *Red River*, but ultimately the film endorses entrepreneurial capitalism' (*ibid.*). Characters in Carpenter's films are also 'distanced from normal legal and social structures,' but the difference is Carpenter's films depict 'those very structures as the locus of corruption' (*ibid.*). Carpenter's protagonists are often outcasts from mainstream society for various reasons. For example, Ethan Bishop's (Austin Stoker) blackness differentiates him from the rest of the police force in *Assault on Precinct 13*, and Nada (Roddy Piper) is left out of luxuries of the elite class because of his working poor status in *They Live* (1988). However, the films quickly reveal that the legal and social structures have been corrupted; the police are mostly worthless in *Precinct 13*, and the elite class in *They Live* is revealed as alien invaders. The ages of Laurie, Annie, and Lynda make them outcasts, cut off by their parents and set adrift in lonely— and deadly—Haddonfield on Halloween night and left to 'face monumental horrors alone' (Cumbow 2000: 54).

The divide between youths and law enforcement is illustrated by a scene that takes place when Annie and Laurie are driving to their babysitting gigs. As Annie and Laurie share a joint, Annie is shocked to see her father with a group of police officers outside of a hardware store downtown. After putting away the joint, the girls pull up to the curb and hear a loud alarm ringing. Raising her voice to be heard above the alarm, Annie asks, 'What happened?':

Brackett:	Someone broke into the hardware store, probably kids.
Annie:	You blame everything on kids.
Brackett:	Well, now, all they took was some Halloween masks, rope, and a couple of knives. Who do you think it was?
Annie (to Laurie):	It's hard growing up with a cynical father.

Carpenter's depiction of the police is more cynical than Brackett could ever hope to be. While the scene offers some comic relief, it also demonstrates that battle lines have been drawn between the young and the establishment in Haddonfield. Annie's complaint that Brackett 'blames everything on kids' suggests that this conflict has arisen many times in the past: something goes wrong, and youths are to blame. As Woods would say, the teens of Haddonfield are 'us,' and the police and adult authorities are 'them.' As Leeder observes, Carpenter creates 'separate spheres of the adolescent and adult,' and the audience 'can see how neatly those lines are divided in *Halloween*' (2014: 75). The ringing alarm makes conversation between Annie and Brackett almost impossible, as if they are speaking two different languages. The sound barrier represents an institutional barrier dividing youths and the police.

If law enforcement is a threat to youth in Haddonfield, however, it is mostly because of incompetence rather than corruption. As a representative of law enforcement, Brackett proves to be ineffectual throughout the film. At the hardware store, Brackett is incorrect about the identity of perpetrator behind the break-in. It is not some anonymous teenage troublemakers who steal the masks, knives, and rope, but Michael, who uses one of the stolen knives to murder Brackett's daughter only a few hours later. As Roche puts it, Brackett 'fails to protect his daughter, her friends, and the community' (2014: 72). Brackett's misidentification of the culprit provides another example of how a Haddonfield institution places its young people in danger with its ineptitude. After Annie and Laurie continue on their ride, Laurie worries that Brackett smelled the joint they were smoking, saying fretfully, 'Think he knew? I'm sure he could smell it. . . . Did you see the look on his face?' Annie scoffs, 'He always looks like that,' confident that her father can be easily fooled. Michael's killing spree takes place completely under the nose of Brackett and the rest of the police force. The Haddonfield police force offers a textbook example of 'failed human intervention' when facing the threat, a trademark of paranoid horror (Tudor 1989: 217). But it is possible that the police force is not entirely to blame for failing to stop Michael since Brackett is given some bad advice from a representative of another failed social institution.

Perhaps the most prominent representative of a failed, corrupt social institution in *Halloween* is Dr. Loomis. Ostensibly, Loomis should be the hero of the film. As Leeder notes, he is 'the film's key figure of patriarchal authority' but 'he, like Brackett, is a failed patriarch' (2014: 76) (see Figure 2.3). He does not exhibit the 'effective expertise' of the authorities in secure horror and offers only 'ineffective expertise' characteristic of paranoid horror (Tudor 1989: 217). Loomis's lack of expertise is observable when he first appears. On the night of 30 October 1978, Loomis and a nurse are driving

Figure 2.3 Brackett and Loomis: Ineffective expertise

to Smith's Grove hospital through the dark and stormy night to transfer Michael to stand trial as an adult. Loomis seems calm and collected, though his words to the nurse are uneasy:

Loomis:	Just try and understand what we're dealing with here. Don't underestimate it.
Nurse:	Don't you think we could refer to 'it' as 'him'?
Loomis:	If you say so.
Nurse (sarcastically):	Your compassion's overwhelming, doctor.

Loomis's reference to Michael as 'it' suggests that he gave up on Michael a long time ago. He later tells Brackett, 'I spent eight years trying to reach him and then another seven trying to keep him locked up because I realized what was living behind that boy's eyes was purely and simply evil.' In Wood's reading of the film as reactionary, Loomis's diagnosis of Michael is key to interpreting the film. Wood believes the film suggests 'the *possibility* [emphasis in original] of psychoanalytical explanation' for Michael's crimes, leaving 'two possible explanations: either he *is* the devil, possessed of supernatural powers; or he has *not* spent the last nine [sic] years . . . staring blankly at a wall meditating further horrors' (1979a: 26). The latter option would suggest Michael's evil is 'what his analyst has been projecting on to him for the past nine [sic] years' (1979a: 26). But Wood feels that the film ultimately agrees with Loomis's character that Michael is inhumanly evil, as opposed to normality's shadow, and trying to read the film against Loomis 'does not constitute a legitimate (let alone coherent) reading of the actual film' (*ibid.*).[7]

This reading is more legitimate and coherent, however, if one considers the broader view of the failure of institutions and how these institutions fail young people in specific. Muir writes:

> The victims of Michael Myers in *Halloween* do not expect to die at the hands of such a monster because they live in what should be a safe society. There is medicine, science, law, education; there is the security blanket of parental protection. In *Halloween*, none of those protections function adequately. Parents are universally absent, the law is completely ineffective, and science has released (but not created) the monster which stalks the streets. Thus teenagers Laurie, Annie, Lynda and Bob have no protection at all from Michael Myers.
>
> (2000: 77)

The parents and educational system in Haddonfield fail the youth. The law does as well, by allowing Michael to escape. He may not have had an opportunity if the law did not arbitrarily dictate that he appear before a judge on his 21st birthday. On the way to Smith's Grove, the nurse asks Loomis why they are going through all of the trouble of taking Michael before a judge if he has no hope of parole, to which Loomis replies, 'Because that is the law,' the tone in his voice suggesting that he agrees the process is perfunctory.[8] Perhaps it only makes sense, then, that the science of psychology fails them as well. Muir notes that science does not create the monster in *Halloween*; it only lets it escape. However, given how incorrect and wrongheaded Loomis is about everything else, the possibility that Smith's Grove made an already disturbed child even worse is not out of the question.

Ultimately, Loomis does not do anything particularly well. He quickly loses his composure at Smith's Grove, snapping at the nurse and running to a call box and leaving her alone. She is immediately attacked by Michael, who steals the car and drives off, leaving a panicked Loomis to impotently exclaim, 'He's gone. He's gone from here. The evil is gone.' A later scene with Dr. Wynn (Robert Phalen), an administrator at Smith's Grove, shows that Loomis was unsuccessful in convincing their officials that Michael was a dangerous patient (which may not have been Loomis's fault, but represents another institutional failure either way). When he arrives in Haddonfield and meets up with Brackett at the hardware store (a scene of law enforcement failure), he fails to see Michael drive by right behind him. When he convinces Brackett to take the threat of Michael seriously, he instructs Brackett to not inform the local news media so as to not cause a panic when awareness of a killer on the loose may have helped. At the old Myers house, Loomis believes Michael will return to the house and elects to wait for him, but Michael never returns. After waiting behind a hedge for over an hour, Loomis looks over his shoulder and notices the station wagon Michael stole from Smith's Grove, which leads one to wonder why it takes Loomis so long to see an automobile parked within eyeshot of where he has been standing for hours.[9] While it is true that lapses in judgement like Loomis's are what make many horror narratives possible as audiences are asked to suspend disbelief the preponderance of institutional failure in the film is overwhelming. If *Halloween* does not, as Wood argues, give the viewer a critique of the bourgeois patriarchal family, perhaps it offers something broader: a cynical appraisal of the systemic shortcomings of dominant ideology as this is personified by its key institutions.

Conclusion

While Wood and Tudor offer two of the most prominent methodological paradigms in the study of horror cinema, this chapter concludes that Tudor's framework produces a more useful reading of *Halloween*. Utilizing a methodology informed by a fusion of ideas derived from the work of Marx and Freud,

Wood reads *Halloween* as an endorsement of bourgeois values, via its depiction of Michael as 'pure evil' rather than as a monster created by repression required to sustain the middle-class, heteronormative family. If the film had depicted the monster not as pure evil but as 'normality's shadow,' one could read it, according to Wood's rubric, as a 'progressive' horror film containing a critique of capitalist patriarchy. Instead, Wood classifies the film as politically 'reactionary,' not only because of its refusal to explore the social forces that shaped Michael into a killer, but also because female characters like Judith, Annie, and Lynda are ostensibly punished for their sexual promiscuity.

Tudor's framework produces a better reading of *Halloween* that draws attention both to Carpenter's critique of social institutions and to the groundwork Carpenter lays for future teen slasher films. Rather than reading the film as a fundamentally conservative text, Tudor's taxonomy of 'secure' versus 'paranoid' horror reveals *Halloween* as a film deeply skeptical of established social institutions because they consistently fail young people. As a result, young people are cut off from any protection adult institutions could offer and left to fend for themselves. As this chapter demonstrates, this scenario is partly essayed through Carpenter's visuals alone. As photographed by Carpenter's team, Haddonfield is an eerily quiet and shadowy place, even in the daytime. Additionally, *Halloween*'s story exposes a whole parade of institutions—education, law, and science—as ineffectual in stopping the threat. In future teen slashers, the separation from adult institutions like the law is often geographic, as teen characters travel to the woods or similar isolated environments and are beset by a killer there. In Haddonfield, young people do not need to go far in order to be isolated; just a step outside the door will suffice. In this way, *Halloween* is both typical and unique of youth horror's depiction of institutional failure.

As this chapter argues, Tudor's model draws out how *Halloween* taps into young people's fears that the institutions that are supposed to nurture, educate, and protect them will ultimately fail them, especially when young people need them the most. As authorities fail and expertise proves ineffectual, Tudor's model of paranoid horror shifts the focus from the experts who should be able to stop the monster to the victims who are forced to face it on their own. The next chapter examines these victims and argues that some of them die not because of their promiscuity but because they betray other members of the group. In an inhospitable place like Haddonfield, teenagers have to watch their backs because adults are unwilling or incapable.

Notes

1 Canadian filmmaker Bob Clark directed this film two years before *Black Christmas*.
2 See Polan (2007).
3 See Britton (1979).

4 These authors are imaginary.
5 This scene is discussed in more detail in Chapter 3.
6 See Paul (1994); Cumbow (2000); Short (2007).
7 Chapter 4 discusses how director Rob Zombie attempts such a reading with his 2007 remake.
8 Chapter 3 discusses the juvenile justice system in more detail.
9 See Leeder (2014: 83–87) for a more detailed discussion of Loomis.

3   A Triptych of Youth

Teenagers, Preadolescents, and Young Adults in *Halloween*

The previous chapter discussed the ways in which *Halloween* resembles the 'paranoid' horror film as described by Andrew Tudor. Many of these 'paranoid' characteristics are among the film's foundational themes: the ineffective expertise of authority figures, the threat that comes from within, and the lack of closure at the narrative's end, with the monster left undefeated. However pertinent all these factors are, the aspect of 'paranoid' horror that is perhaps most prominent in *Halloween* is the focus on the victim group. Tudor explains that in 'secure' horror, there is a 'centre-periphery structure. Those at the centre are conventionally expected to be capable of autonomous action; those at the periphery require the protection of centrally located expertise' (1989: 215). 'Paranoid' horror reverses this schema. Since the authorities and the experts cannot defeat the monster or protect those on the periphery, the focus shifts to the victim group, left to fend for themselves. In *Halloween*, this victim group is made up of young people who are abandoned at the periphery by Haddonfield's center: its adults and social institutions.

The victim group in any horror film is important, but the young people in *Halloween* occupy a significant place in horror cinema history because they constitute the victim group in what is generally considered to be the progenitor of the slasher film. The teen slasher film came along after a quarter century of profitable youth horror films, and catering to this audience made young people the 'prime movie-going demographic' (Nowell 2011: 34). In the past, horror films for youth audiences did not always feature young people, but in slasher films, they became an essential component, comprising the majority of the victim group. As Richard Nowell puts it, 'On screen depictions of the target audience were perhaps the most valuable hooks' that a film targeted at youth audiences could have (36). Understanding the value of this hook, Carpenter and Hill prioritized the veracity of *Halloween*'s youth characters. The film's success suggests *Halloween*'s youth characters connected with audiences.

Teenagers are not the only engaging youth characters in the film, as it also features preadolescents and young adults in compelling roles. If as Nowell argues, on screen depictions of the target audience were a valuable hook in the youth film market, the presence of preadolescent characters suggests that the makers of *Halloween* may have had their eye on youth audiences outside the teenage demographic. Yablans believed that slasher films were highly appealing to pre-teens, and in a 1980 interview, Yablans notes that kids from ages 11 to 12 have the 'greatest response' to teen slasher movies (quoted in Nowell 2011: 40). He thought his 'Babysitter Murders' idea would be appealing because 'everybody had either been a babysitter or been a baby' (Anchor Bay 2013b), with his comment about everyone having 'been a baby' suggesting *Halloween*'s appeal beyond the teenage audience. Another dimension of *Halloween*'s depiction of youth is how Michael Myers embodies the young adult. The film's opening tempts one to think of 21-year-old Michael (erroneously identified in the credits as being 23 years old)[1] as an overgrown child, the fixed stare on his 6-year-old face after he murders Judith suggesting he will remain frozen in time. However, details in the film identify Michael as a young adult, broken by a failed criminal justice system and resisting the responsibilities of becoming an adult. The roles played by preadolescents and young adults in *Halloween* contribute to the film's multifaceted depiction of youth and bears closer examination.

The objective of this chapter is to illustrate how *Halloween*'s youth characters are more complex and richer than they may first appear. While Clover's concept of the 'Final Girl' has proven useful in slasher film analysis, this chapter contends that relying on this mode of analysis runs the risk of overlooking other members of the victim group, besides the Final Girl, who may be equally compelling. This chapter instead examines the core teenage group as examples of the character types that 'permeate the subgenre' of 'youth in school' movies (Shary 2014: 34–35), looking at Laurie as the 'nerd,' Annie as the 'rebel,' and Lynda as the 'popular girl.' This approach unveils nuanced aspects of the girls' relationship and offers insight into what goes wrong in their relationship to allow in a destructive interloper like Michael.

This chapter also examines the film's two preadolescent characters, Tommy and Lindsay. While the depiction of teenagers in the film is focused on female characters, this chapter holds that the opposite is true of the preadolescent duo, as Tommy is the one who has a discernable character arc. Finally, this chapter examines Michael as a youth character, considering him as a young adult. This approach reveals Michael as a figure broken by a failed criminal justice system—another example of institutional failure in the film—and unable to enter the adult world. Ultimately, the chapter argues that, while it cannot lay claim to being the first slasher film, *Halloween* provides a range of character types from which future slasher films would draw.

The Teenage Trinity: Laurie, Annie, and Lynda

One of the factors that led Yablans to commission a female teen-centric horror screenplay from Carpenter and Hill was the box office success of *Carrie* two years previous, and some have compared *Halloween*'s characters to those in *Carrie*, drawing conclusions about the characters in *Halloween* that diverge and converge. Timothy Shary opines that *Halloween* 'evacuate[s] the expansive subgenre [of youth horror] of the character development seen in *Carrie*' (2005: 57). According to Shary, Carpenter's film '[does] not provide much background on the featured characters other than their ages, their senses of hedonism or puritanism (the four who are murdered have or are planning to have sex, and the survivor is dutifully babysitting), and their ignorance to the danger at hand' (2014: 163–164). Danny Peary feels differently. Writing in 1981, Peary calls Laurie, Annie, and Lynda some of 'the most believable teenagers' in film and writes, '[I]t's a real treat watching these three Middle America teenagers jabber away about boys, school, dates, sex, etc. They are witty . . . smart . . . and odd in a conventional way' (1981: 125). While Shary feels the characters in *Carrie* are more fully realized, Peary argues that *Carrie* exudes a 'hostility toward teenage girls' that is absent in *Halloween* (*ibid.*). Shary and Peary do agree on one thing, however: the deaths of the sexually active girls and the survival of the dutiful babysitter are problematic elements of *Halloween*. Shary's description of the film's characters seems to divide them neatly into punished hedonists and rewarded puritans (2014: 163), and Peary denounces the film's 'puritanical "morality"' (1981: 126).

Both of these viewpoints need nuance. Early academic analysis of the slasher film by scholars such as Clover and Dika proposes that teenagers in slasher films—including those in *Halloween*—can be neatly divided into guilty victims and virginal survivors (Clover 1987; Dika 1990), but in many slasher films, these divisions are not clear cut. Complex characterizations are a part of the slasher film from the beginning. For instance, Clover argues that the 'Final Girl,' that is, the boyish, virginal character who is rewarded for her 'purity' by surviving until the end, is a staple of slasher cinema. However, if one considers *Black Christmas* as the first slasher, Jess (Oliva Hussey), a young woman pregnant by her unstable boyfriend (Keir Dullea) and considering the termination of both the pregnancy and the relationship, does not resemble the typical Final Girl.

Even though *Halloween*'s Laurie Strode more closely resembles the typical Final Girl, *Halloween*'s characters are also more complex than they may first appear, and the film's group of teenagers merits examination that goes beyond classifying them as hedonistic or puritanical. While Peary is correct that *Halloween* is bereft of the monstrous female bullies of *Carrie*, there are tensions among the group that cause them to fracture during a time of crisis. The victim group in *Halloween* is a teenage version of the type of groups that find themselves under siege in Carpenter's other films, which often feature a 'small, enclosed community . . . pitted against a seemingly irresistible and relentless external force that is bent on its destruction' (Smith 2004: 36). In films like *Assault on Precinct 13* and *Prince of Darkness* (1987), Carpenter's ragtag communities stick together and overcome the threat. However, *Halloween* finds itself among films like Carpenter's *The Thing*, in which the group is too fragmented to defeat the threat. These fissures in *Halloween*'s victim group make the film a more nuanced presentation of youth than its spartan plot suggests, as it depicts the ways in which young people must navigate a hostile world in which their cohort both supports and disappoints them. Before proceeding to a more detailed examination of each member of *Halloween*'s central trio, the Final Girl must be addressed, if for no other reason, because she is likely the most well-known character archetype of the teen slasher.

Final Things First: Laurie as Prototypical 'Final Girl'

Coined by Clover in 1987, the Final Girl is the rarest of creatures: a piece of academic jargon that made its way into popular culture vernacular. Clover observes that most slasher films feature a female protagonist who is the last one left after all members of the victim group have been killed off. This young woman survives long enough for help to arrive, or she defeats the killer herself. Either way, she is the Final Girl, the last of the teen victim group left alive. Clover notes that the Final Girl is differentiated from the rest of the victim group in several ways. She is 'presented from the outset as the main character' and is 'the only character to be developed in any psychological detail' (2015: 88, 92). Unlike her friends, the Final Girl is a bookish wallflower who is not sexually active (88).

Clover explores the possible function the Final Girl plays for slasher film audiences, whom she assumes are mostly male. At first, the audience sees the plot unfold from the perspective (the 'I-camera') of the killer, which is coded as male (92). As the plot progresses, however, the perspective shifts from the killer to the Final Girl, as the audience roots for her to defeat the killer, a process Clover calls 'cross-gender identification' (93). Throughout this process, the gender of both the killer and the Final Girl are fluid. From the outset, both characters have masculine and feminine characteristics. For instance, the Final Girl often possesses 'boyish' qualities, one of which is her virginity; Clover argues that any sort of penetration would make her too uncomfortably feminine to act as a 'congenial double for the adolescent male' (99). On the flipside, the killer's virginity represents a lack of virility that threatens to make him feminine. When the Final Girl wrests phallic power away from the killer and defeats him in the end, she satisfies the male audience because she has 'not just manned herself . . . [S]he unmans an oppressor whose masculinity was in question to begin with' (96). At the same time, however, her femininity also plays an important role in this process. Since she is a female character, the Final Girl is allowed to cry, whimper, and scream in abject terror, displaying emotions men are forbidden to express in patriarchal culture (96–97). Thus, the young male spectators sublimate their fears and anxieties about growing up as the Final Girl makes the harrowing journey from fearfully feminine childhood to the masculine mastery of adulthood in their place. Clover's article framed academic discourse surrounding the slasher film for many years.

Clover's taxonomy seems to align with *Halloween*, and Laurie, the bookish and sexually hesitant main character of the film, seems the ideal example of Clover's Final Girl. As the first character the audience encounters when the film opens on present-day Haddonfield, she is marked as the main character. Shortly after her character is introduced, Michael sees her as she runs an errand at the old Myers house and fixates on her, signaling that she will be his main target. The film also stresses her bookish characteristics. When called on in the classroom, Laurie answers the teacher's question with ease (even though a masked man lurking around outside the window spooks her), leaving little doubt about her acumen as a student. As she and her friends walk home from school, Laurie carries a huge pile of books, and Lynda pokes fun at her: 'Oh, look at you! Look at all the books you have! You need a shopping cart to get home!' Her intelligence interferes with her love life, however. In regards to her lack of dates, Laurie says, 'Guys think I'm too smart.' While Laurie is not 'boyish' (outside of her implied virginity), she neatly fits Clover's description of the typical Final Girl. The confrontation between Laurie and Michael fits Clover's schema as well; in fact, Clover uses Laurie's defeat of Michael as the example of the struggle for phallic power that takes place between the Final Girl and the killer (96). In a 1980 interview, Carpenter seems to foreshadow Clover's hypothesis: '[Laurie's] the one that's killed him . . . because all the repressed sexual energy starts coming out. She uses all those phallic symbols on the guy' (quoted in McCarthy 1980: 23–24). Indeed, it is difficult to overlook the phallic nature of Michael's attacks on his victims and how Laurie turns this power against him by penetrating him with a knitting needle, a hanger, and his own knife (see Figure 3.1). Clover says Laurie's penetration of Michael stands in for the sex act for the male viewer, who is now inaugurated into manhood via the Final Girl.

Figure 3.1 Laurie, the final girl

While Clover's formula offers a useful mode of analysis, there are several blind spots in her argument, and addressing these blind spots forces a consideration of the representation of youth in *Halloween*—specifically, its representation of girlhood—from a different perspective. As discussed in Chapter 1, Nowell notes that 'there are . . . several economic factors that point to the figure of the dynamic and heroic female being mobilized to appeal . . . to female youth' in the first slasher film cycle (2011: 128). Clover's argument is predicated on a majority of the slasher film's audience being male, which Nowell's research demonstrates was not the case; great pains were taken by slasher film producers to appeal to female audiences, whose business was necessary for box office success. This drive to attract female audiences would only increase as the slasher film cycle took off after the release of *Friday the 13th*. Nowell points out that a majority of heroines from these teen slashers—like *Prom Night* and *Hell Night* (DeSimone, 1981)—are quite different from the image of the virginal tomboy as described by Clover. Actually, the teen slasher most often featured 'heroines that exhibited an abundance of traditionally feminine traits' (207).

When Clover considers female slasher audiences in her analysis, she hypothesizes that perhaps 'females respond to the text (the literal) and males the subtext (the figurative)' (2015: 101). Even if this is the case, the text is still worth examination since the text shows the plot and story elements filmmakers utilized to attract female audiences (Nowell 2011: 70). As such, it may be best at this point to depart from an analysis of the Final Girl, if only because its focus on the virginal survivor runs the risk of dismissing other female characters in the film as expendable bimbos. The next section, focusing on Laurie in relation to Annie and Lynda, argues that, far from being one-dimensional fodder for Michael's knife, Annie and Lynda are more complicated than they first seem. Rather than focusing on Laurie as the Final Girl in relation to the killer, this section will begin by considering Laurie as a 'nerd,' a stereotypical character from the school film, in order to unveil her relationship with Annie and Lynda and place her in a wider context of the film's teen characters, those literal elements of the films that female audiences may enjoy most.

A Nerd Triumphant: Laurie Strode

Shary's taxonomy of common character types in films featuring youths in a school setting provides a useful framework for examining *Halloween*'s teens. Shary argues that school films feature characters that generally fall into one of five categories: the nerd, the delinquent, the rebel, the 'popular' type, and the athlete (2014: 34). The boundaries between these categories are often challenged during the course of a film's narrative, but they are crossed and/or maintained only through great effort. Nerds must undertake challenging journeys to be accepted by the popular crowd. Popular kids must work hard to maintain their privileged position in the social hierarchy. Laurie, Annie, and Lynda resemble the nerd, rebel, and 'popular' types, respectively. However, *Halloween* is an atypical school film in that only three scenes (all discussed in the previous chapter) take place in a school setting. Outside of the school setting, the girls' roles are less fixed, creating a sense of fluidity as the nerd, rebel, and popular type interact with each other across social categories. These border crossings make *Halloween*'s teens more nuanced than they may initially appear.

Laurie, whom Clover would refer to as the Final Girl, often resembles the nerd character type from 1980s school films, and focusing on Laurie as a nerd rather than a Final Girl allows one to appreciate her in relation to her other friends, not to the killer. Other teen characters poke fun at nerds for 'blatant conformity to institutional expectations' (37). Laurie strives to meet expectations both inside and outside the classroom. The load of books she totes home from school suggests that she excels in school. Outside of academics, she also strives to be a perfect babysitter. When babysitting Tommy, Laurie brings a pumpkin, telling Annie that she plans to carve a jack-o-lantern, the perfect, sanctioned Halloween activity. Annie quips, 'I always said you'd make a fabulous girl scout.' Annie's wisecracks aside, Laurie is evidently babysitter extraordinaire, as evidenced by Tommy's excitement to be spending Halloween night with her. That morning, he excitedly rushes up to her to barrage her with questions about what activities they will do that night. Laurie clearly exceeds expectations at school and on the job. In their pursuit of institutional perfection, nerds are often made fun of, picked on, or bullied by fellow students, but things play out differently in *Halloween*.

Laurie's character arc differs from the typical character trajectory of nerds in school films. Shary argues that 'in many ways, nerds face the greatest struggle of all school characters because they must make the most forceful denials of their true nature' (*ibid.*). Conversely, Laurie never denies her true nature as she strives to be an excellent student and the best babysitter in town. Her focus on the job saves her life and, potentially, the lives of the children she watches over. Immediately after *Halloween*'s release, many commentators accused the film of conservatism since the character who performs her traditionally assigned 'womanly duties' (namely, keeping the household and watching the children) survives while the other, sexually active characters are killed (Wood 1979a: 26; Rosenbaum 1979). However, Humphries suggests that the cinematic 'girl of eighteen [who wishes] to give priority to her studies over sex' is the true non-conformist (2002: 140). Similarly, Sue Short argues the slasher film is not 'an attempt to regulate female sexuality' but rather 'a positive affirmation of female capability [and] non-conformity' whose 'characterisation extols self-realisation above conformity' (2007: 46). Laurie is a self-realized nerd who breaks from the conventions of the run-of-the-mill school film. Shary observes that the only 'option for all nerds' is 'change or perish' (2014: 37), but Laurie bucks this convention. She survives because she does not change.

Even though Laurie is a triumphant nerd, her agency is equivocated, but even this shortcoming ultimately works to her advantage. To keep the nerdy girl's intelligence from becoming too intimidating for male characters, school films often 'alleviate [her smarts] through other liabilities,' one of which is often 'shyness' (38). Indeed, Laurie's shyness and demure nature temper the threat of her intelligence. As Laurie and Annie discuss Laurie's lack of a love life, Annie declares, 'It's tragic. You never go out. You must have a small fortune stashed away from babysitting so much.' Laurie meekly responds, 'Guys think I'm too smart.' However, one may hear a hint of jealousy in Annie's voice when she speculates that Laurie could possibly have stashed away some disposable income—that most cherished item of a teenager's world—because of babysitting duties. Thus, Laurie's timidity places her in a position where intelligence has forced her into hard work that has paid off, turning her weakness into a strength. Miriam Forman-Brunell argues that Laurie's 'autonomy [as a] female income [earner]' makes her a 'transgressor' in patriarchal society (2002: 258). Perhaps Laurie's transgressive nature explains why she is best friends with *Halloween*'s rebel, Annie.

She's a Rebel: Annie Brackett

Out of the main trio of teenagers, Annie is the rebel. Annie may not immediately strike one as a rebel, but as Shary observes, the rebel is a 'more heterogeneous' character type than others in the school film, appearing in many permutations (2014: 60). The fact that Annie's father is the sheriff of Haddonfield brings another dimension to Annie's rebelliousness. In several school films, rebels embody 'demonstrative anger that seems to come from the ignorance of wealthy parents' (61). While Annie is not 'angry' exactly, nor does she come from a wealthy family (being a police officer is most often not a lucrative enterprise), a dynamic similar to this type of relationship is at play between dope-smoking Annie and Sheriff Brackett. As discussed in the previous chapter, law enforcement is one of many institutions that fails Haddonfield's young people and leaves them in peril, so it stands to reason that the child of the sheriff would be the most disenchanted and cynical of the group.

Annie's rebellious nature is clear from her first appearance as the trio of girls walk home from school. Michael drives by in the station wagon he stole from Smith's Grove. He slows to a crawl as he passes, his shadowy head craning to take a long look. The girls react to this moment in accordance with their character types. Laurie is alert, being the first to notice the car—the moment she sees it is emphasized as Carpenter's theme begins to play—and is nervous because she saw the car outside school earlier. Lynda mistakes Michael for a male classmate whom she finds attractive, asking 'Hey, isn't that Devon Graham? . . . I think he's cute.' Irritated, Annie yells at the car, 'Hey jerk! Speed kills!' Michael slams on the brakes and, with a loud screech, brings the car to a halt. The girls are shaken by this abrupt action and take a step back, in anticipation of what the driver may do next. Annie is the first one to rebound and shift back into sarcastic mode, scoffing 'God, can't he take a joke?' Laurie nervously scolds her, 'You know, Annie, someday you're going to get us all in deep trouble,' but Annie will not let up, quipping, 'I hate a guy with a car and no sense of humor.' Annie does not change her demeanor for anyone, nor will she be silenced by anything, including potential threats.

A careful look at the relationship between Annie and Laurie brings out the richness of Annie's characterization. Studies of the slasher film often write off characters like Annie and Lynda as one-dimensional social types and focus instead on binary relationships between the Final Girl and her friends or the Final Girl and the killer (Dika 1990: 46–52). However, exact binaries are difficult to come by in *Halloween* due to the permeable social boundaries between character types in Haddonfield. Annie's cocky attitude, pot smoking, and active sexuality might suggest that she falls on an entirely opposite side of the social spectrum as someone like nerdy Laurie, but there are many ways in which the two overlap. During the girls' walk home from school, a small detail in the *mise-en-scène* suggests Laurie and Annie are not entirely dissimilar. Laurie carries a stack of textbooks, but Annie carries only one less than Laurie, as a bookless Lynda jokes, 'Oh, who needs books anyway?' Annie is closer to Laurie on the intellectual spectrum, casting into doubt the notion that Laurie is the binary opposite of her friends. Another thing Annie and Laurie have in common is that they are babysitters, even if they approach the vocation in extremely dissimilar ways. Laurie takes a wholesome, interactive approach to babysitting; she reads to Tommy, engages in various activities with him, and chides him, in a motherly way, for reading comic books that he has hidden from his parents. On the other hand, Annie's approach is more hands-off and self-centered; she plants Lindsey on the couch in front of the television so she can talk on the phone.

Annie's babysitting techniques become another manifestation of her rebellion. Shary notes that rebels 'are best defined by what they do not want to do—conform—but if they are going to make it in society (or school) they must find some means of surviving with their adamant individuality intact, which necessitates the sophistication of their techniques' (2014: 60). This process describes Annie's efforts to rebel while still functioning within larger societal structures. Sexual rebellion is Annie's primary motivation, as she refuses to conform to the ideology of pre-marriage abstinence. She uses her babysitting gigs as an opportunity to hook up with her boyfriend, trysting in the bedrooms of unsuspecting couples trusting enough to leave their children under her care. As Lynda puts it, the 'only reason [Annie] babysits is to have a place to . . .' but is cut off before she can presumably say 'fuck.' While her plan may be crude, Annie makes it work, as she apparently amassed a great deal of sexual experience. When Laurie jokes that Annie and Paul were 'exploring uncharted territory' in the boys' locker room, Lynda responds, 'It's been totally charted.' Later, when Paul jokes that sex is all Annie thinks about, she declares, 'That's not true. I think about lots of things. Now why don't we not stand here talking about them and get down to doing them?' Annie has mastered her domain. Her sophisticated technique allows her to seemingly conform while retaining her rebellious individuality, as she uses the babysitting business and all its attendant heteronormative practices of child-rearing and domestic maintenance to cloak her sexual escapades.

Annie's ability to shift gears and switch between different identities has allowed her to thrive as a rebel in Haddonfield. There are several instances of Annie's expert transformations in the film. For instance, when Annie and Laurie are driving along and sharing a joint, they run across Sheriff Brackett investigating a break-in at the hardware store. Annie seems to lose her cool, but only for a moment. She quickly recovers, instructs a coughing Laurie to 'be natural,' and pulls up to her father, calmly and confidently. She even cracks a couple of jokes at his expense. Annie exhibits similar dexterity on the job. When Paul manages to sneak out of his parents' home, Annie tells Lindsey that they are going to pick him up, but Lindsey resists. Irritated, Annie says, 'Look Lindsey, I thought we understood each other.' This exchange insinuates that Annie has carefully rehearsed and executed this subterfuge with Lindsey before. Lindsey's stubbornness poses a roadblock for Annie, but she quickly steers around it, asking Lindsey if she would like to watch television with Tommy and enticing her over to the Doyle residence, which leaves Laurie looking after both kids while Annie goes to pick up Paul. Annie uses information gleaned from Laurie earlier in the evening to bribe her into watching Lindsey, another bit of finesse that allows Annie to pursue her own pleasure. Annie has the ability to maneuver and never lets her guard down for long.

However, Annie does open up during an exchange with Laurie in an earlier scene that may be the emotional center of *Halloween*. After their encounter with Sheriff Brackett, the sun begins to set, and the two have a conversation about the upcoming homecoming dance. Several visual cues suggest that this exchange is of a different nature than ones earlier in the drive. Up to this point, Carpenter shoots the car trip as a medium shot taken from a camera mounted on the front of the car, which allows the viewer to see both Annie and Laurie through the windshield (see Figure 3.2). Interspersed throughout this master shot are cuts to medium close-ups on Annie and Laurie to emphasize specific moments in their conversation. Carpenter deviates from this three-shot pattern only twice with two shots taken from within the cab of the car: one shot out the back window shows Michael's station wagon following them, unbeknownst to the girls, and another shot taken from Annie's POV as they pull up to the hardware store to talk with Sheriff Brackett. For the most part, however, Carpenter sticks with the three-shot pattern looking through the car's windshield.

Figure 3.2 Annie and Laurie drive to the job

Thus, when the camera significantly changes position and proximity to the characters, the visual shift alone creates a different mood.[2] The camera sits in the back seat, shooting Annie and Laurie from behind. A master shot captures the back of their heads in a medium close-up. Then, the sequence settles into a shot/reverse shot pattern, cutting back and forth between close-ups of Annie and Laurie at 45-degree angles looking over their shoulders. The close-ups capture them in profile, which sometimes suggests aloofness, but here the proximity conveys intimacy in Annie and Laurie's friendship. There is level of trust between them because Laurie allows herself to be vulnerable here—a brave feat when dealing with a sarcastic cynic like Annie—and Annie responds with what seems like genuine support. Laurie asks Annie what she plans to wear to the dance. Annie replies, 'I didn't know you thought about things like that, Laurie' in her typical, teasing tone. Laurie sits silently, glancing down at her lap. She then raises her eyes back to Annie with a look of embarrassed longing, then looks back down. Laurie's silence and sad expression cause Annie to shift to an encouraging tone, saying, 'You know, you could ask somebody. . . . All you have to do is go up to somebody and say, "Do you wanna go to the dance?"' While there is a hint of jocularity in Annie's voice, this moment is the closest she comes to being nurturing in the film. The sunlight coming through the windshield makes her look almost angelic (see Figure 3.3). The conversation soon moves back to the usual tone, with Annie teasing Laurie when she expresses romantic interest in a classmate named Ben Tramer, but all the visual elements—the proximity of the camera, the growing darkness in the car as day turns to night, the sunset shining through the windshield and creating lens flares and dappling the actors with bits of orange sunlight—give weight to this fleeting moment of connection.

Figure 3.3 Annie's advice

The Labor of Popularity: Lynda

Neither Annie nor Laurie share a similar moment with Lynda, a character who, out of the main trio of girls in *Halloween*, adheres most closely with a recognizable character type in the typical school film: that of the 'popular' girl. Unlike Annie and Laurie, Lynda is not a babysitter, but that does not mean she is not hard at work. She is busy with the task of being popular. Lives of popular kids in school movies may seem effortless, but there is 'the great effort involved in maintaining' the status of being popular (Shary 2014: 74). The labor of being popular is noted early on in *Halloween*. Lynda exits the school with Laurie and complains:

> You know, it's totally insane. We have three new cheers to learn in the morning, the game is in the afternoon, I have to get my hair done at five, and the dance is at eight! I'll be totally wiped out!

Laurie jokes, 'I don't think you have enough to do tomorrow,' to which Lynda replies, 'Totally!' According to Lynda, being popular is exhausting work. Lynda's challenge of transforming from cheerleader into dancing queen demonstrates how 'popular students must appear and act acceptable to a wide range of people' (73).

Lynda boasts other features of the popular girl character type in terms of looks and attitude (*ibid.*). She possesses the beauty of a typical popular girl. Her long blonde hair and tall, slender frame set her apart from Laurie and Annie. Lynda also has expensive taste in clothes. When Bob seductively says he is going to rip her clothes off, Lynda pushes him away, yelling 'Don't rip my blouse! It's expensive, idiot!' Lynda's taste seems to square with Shary's observation that popular girls in film 'usually come from wealthy back-grounds' (75).[3] The viewer learns little about Lynda's family—other than she has a little brother—but her expensive blouse hints that she may come from a well-off family, as does the fact that she does not seem to have a babysitting job. For the most part, Lynda has the 'agreeable attitude' that Shary notices in many popular kids in the movies (73). As played by Soles, Lynda is a lovable character. Her winsome nature is epitomized by her constant use of the word 'totally,' which she peppers into her conversations to express a wide array of emotions, ranging from exclamatory ('I'll be totally wiped out!') to mischie-vous (her chuckling 'totally' to Bob after they drunkenly outline a plan to hook up) to angry (her 'totally' in support of Laurie's comment that Annie's snarky attitude is going to get them into trouble one day) to orgasmic (her breathy 'that was fantastic . . . totally' after having sex with Bob). Lynda's quirks and foibles separate her from popular girls in films who are sometimes ultimately revealed to be mean and full of 'ignorance and conceit' (76).

Figure 3.4 'See anything you like?'

Lynda also gets to enjoy more deviance than some other popular girls, even though she is still putting up appearances during these good times. While some popular girls merely '[long] to be deviant' (75), Lynda drinks beer and has sex with Bob in the upstairs bedroom of the Wallace house. However, one could argue that this sex is actually more performance, as Lynda appears to climax after only a few seconds. Afterwards, Lynda demands that Bob fetch a beer for her. As Bob is on this errand, Michael attacks him in the kitchen, pinning him to the wall by running him through with a butcher knife.[4] Then, Michael, covered in a white sheet and wearing Bob's glasses, goes upstairs to Lynda who believes that it is Bob that is under the sheet. As he stands silent in the doorway, Lynda exposes her breasts and playfully asks, 'See anything you like' (see Figure 3.4)? Ever the popular girl, Lynda continues to work. She offers her body to the gaze, playing the role of sensual spectacle for both Bob/Michael and the viewer. Even when in bed post-coitus, Lynda is still on the job.

Betrayal and Miscommunication: The Trinity Is Broken

Laurie, Annie, and Lynda are busy with the task of being teenage girls in Haddonfield. Laurie has her hands full with school and babysitting. Annie balances a babysitting career with sexual autonomy. Lynda's labor to be popular extends from the ballfield to the bedroom. Haddonfield can be an inhospitable place for young people, but they are making it work. The girls resemble ragtag groups in Carpenter's other films. These groups are often made up of outsiders, isolated from society at large, but when a threat emerges, these loners can often band together and overcome it. However, in some of Carpenter's films, 'the threat . . . isolates the members of the group rather than brings them together' (Grant 2004: 13). *Halloween* is an example of this type of Carpenter film. Initially, the three girls get along, even though they come from different social strata, but there are fissures in the group that worsen when Michael sneaks into their lives. The group splinters and leaves Laurie, the most beleaguered member of the group, isolated.

Early micro-aggressions aimed at Laurie foreshadow the group's dissolution. After Lynda complains about her day packed with social commitments, Laurie dejectedly says, 'As usual I have nothing to do.' Lynda curtly replies, 'It's your own fault and I don't feel a bit sorry for you.' Annie rags on Laurie's lack of a romantic life. When Laurie sees Michael lurking behind a hedge, Annie investigates and finds nothing. She teases, 'Laurie dear, he wants to talk to you. He wants to take you out tonight.' When Laurie sees no one is there, Annie mockingly chides, 'Poor Laurie. Scared another one away.' Later, on the phone, Annie tells Laurie she's 'losing it' because she keeps seeing someone stalking her. Laurie says she has already 'lost it,' to which Annie replies, 'Doubt that,' mocking Laurie's virginity. Something prophetic happens during the beginning of that phone call. Laurie sees Michael out the back window of her house, standing amongst bedsheets pinned to clotheslines and flapping in the wind. Laurie slowly backs away from the window and is surprised by a ringing phone. Shaken, Laurie answers it, hears nothing but indistinct, wet-sounding noises, and slams down the phone. It immediately rings again. Laurie picks it up, and on the other end, Annie asks, 'Why'd you hang up on me?' Annie explains that she was eating and could not speak. Laurie says she thought it was an obscene phone call, and Annie exclaims, 'Now you're hearing obscene chewing! You're losing it, Laurie.' This communication breakdown between Laurie and Annie foreshadows how the group will be lethally infiltrated through division and increasing isolation.

The solidarity of the group dissolves when Annie betrays Laurie's trust. After Paul calls asking Annie to pick him up, Annie asks Laurie to cover for her and take care of Lindsey. Laurie resists, but Annie blackmails her, weaponizing Laurie's earlier confession about Ben Tramer. It turns out Annie has already told Ben about Laurie's crush, much to Laurie's mortification. She groans, 'Oh Annie, please tell me you didn't. How could you do that? . . . I can't tell you anything.' To get Laurie to watch Lindsey so she can hook up with Paul, she bribes Laurie, telling her that if she agrees to watch Lindsey she will '*consider* talking to Ben Tramer in the morning' and let Laurie off the hook. Annie's impromptu plan to hook up with Paul leads her to betray Laurie and take advantage of her. This exchange resembles the type of relationship one may see in typical school films which often find 'cool' kids 'exploit[ing] nerds' skills' (Shary 2014: 37). This type of exchange usually involves the cool kids getting nerds to do their homework or tutor them in a particular subject, but since *Halloween* mostly takes place outside the school in a world preoccupied with work, Annie exploits Laurie's vocational skills.

Visual cues juxtapose this scene of betrayal with an earlier scene of trust when Laurie tells Annie about her crush. In that scene, Annie and Laurie are shot in profile from the shady backseat of the car with the sunset through the windshield backlighting their profile. Now, as Annie teases Laurie about Ben, they stand in a doorframe entering the kitchen of the Doyle house. The camera, placed in an unlit dining room, captures Annie and Laurie in a medium close-up, with backlight emanating from the kitchen. As in the earlier scene, the girls are shot in profile and lit from the back. However, the secret shared in the earlier scene is now exploited, distancing Annie and Laurie. As if to acknowledge this shift, they move positions. Annie walks off screen to the left on her way to the door, and the camera pans with Laurie as she follows. They pause to share a few more words. They are framed by the entryway into the Doyles' dining room. The camera remains in the dining room, but this time, Annie and Laurie are lit from the back by a lamp in the living room. A more significant difference, however, is the change in distance between the characters. In the first set up, they are inches from each other, so close that Annie places a piece of popcorn in Laurie's mouth without fully extending her arm. In the second set up, now in a medium shot, they stand about a meter from each other (see Figure 3.5). There are no acrimonious words—in fact, Laurie seems relieved that her crush on Ben Tramer will now remain a secret—but the placement of the characters suggests Annie's betrayal places distance between them, distance enough, at least, for Michael to infiltrate. He kills Annie when she gets in the car. Michael could have attacked many times before, but he does not strike until the group fragments, when one member betrays and takes advantage of another.

Figure 3.5 Space between friends

With the bond between Laurie and Annie severed, the circle is destroyed, so when Lynda and Bob arrive at the Wallace house, drunk and horny, their deaths are *a fait accompli*. When they realize no one is home, Lynda calls the Doyle house, and Laurie answers. Lynda asks, 'What's up?' Exhausted, Laurie sighs, 'I'm just sitting down for the first time tonight.' Lynda flippantly giggles in response and moves on to other business, not bothered by Laurie's imbalanced workload, and she and Bob are murdered shortly thereafter. The fates of Annie and Lynda seem to confirm Shary's claim that the pleasure of teenage girls in 1970s cinema is often 'ultimately destructive' (2005: 51). Many have read the fates of Annie and Lynda as evidence of the slasher film's punishment of female sexuality, but it is equally possible that Annie and Lynda die because they pursue their own self-interests at Laurie's expense, thereby causing the dissolution of the group. After all, in Carpenter's films, the group must stick together if they hope to defeat the threat. Considering *Halloween* in the context of Carpenter's *oeuvre* produces a reading that runs contrary to assessments of the slasher film that condemn the death of characters like Annie and Lynda as punishment for their sexuality. Annie and Lynda do not die because they break patriarchal society's rules; rather, they die because their actions undermine the solidarity of the (all-female) group.

Lynda's murder completes a circle of miscommunication that isolates each member of the group and allows Michael to infiltrate their ranks. When Michael enters the bedroom under a sheet, Lynda assumes he is Bob and jokes with him. However, Michael does not react; his silence symbolizes how the communication loop among the group has been disrupted. Frustrated by Bob-Michael's silence, Lynda turns to the phone and calls Laurie. Behind her back, Michael creeps up behind her, his incremental movements accentuated by Carpenter's score. When Laurie answers, Michael suddenly wraps the phone cord around Lynda's throat and begins to strangle her. Laurie can only hear Lynda's muffled shrieks. Thinking it is a prank call, Laurie asks, 'All right, Annie, first I get your famous chewing, now I get your famous squealing?' referring to the earlier scene when Laurie is unable to hear Annie on the phone. These two scenes bookend the group's deterioration as Michael corrodes their ability to communicate. The prominence of the phone in these scenes underscores the terror of broken communication. In babysitting stories ranging from urban legends to film to young adult fiction, the telephone often emerges as a 'symbolic threat' (Forman-Brunell 2002: 258), a connotation Debra Hill had in mind when writing the film. She explains that she wanted to explore the 'irony' of how 'the very thing that teenage girls know and love best, which is the telephone, becomes an instrument of death' (Anchor Bay 2013a).

The failure of the phone to connect corresponds with Michael's emergence as a monster. Earlier, before Laurie is unable to hear Annie, she sees

Figure 3.6 Michael, miscommunication, and murder

Michael outside the window. He stands by a clothesline with ghostly sheets flapping around him and disappears before Laurie's eyes. As Michael stifles Lynda's screams, she pulls the sheet off of him, revealing the first close-up of Michael's masked visage as he places the receiver up to his ear and listens to Laurie (see Figure 3.6). As such, the bookend scenes depict Michael in ghostly armaments. He disappears into the clothesline, becoming immaterial long enough to impede the girls' communication, then rematerializes after causing enough static in the telephone line to disrupt communication between the girls.

Preadolescence and Maturation: Tommy and Lindsey

While the teenage group at least begins in solidarity, no such camaraderie ever exists in the preadolescent group, as made clear by Tommy's tribulations. The viewer first encounters Tommy when he sees Laurie on the way to school and asks about their plans for the evening. Laurie reciprocates Tommy's fondness, showing he has a good relationship with someone outside his age group. Tommy's relationships within his youth group, however, are not so pleasant. When Laurie stops to drop off a key at the Myers house for her realtor father, Tommy warns her not to go near the house because it is haunted, information Tommy gleaned from Lonnie Elam (Brent Le Page), a schoolmate: 'Lonnie Elam said never to go up there. Lonnie Elam said that's a haunted house. He said awful stuff happened there once.' Laurie dismisses Lonnie as someone who 'probably won't get out of the sixth grade,' but Lonnie is not so easy to dismiss in person. Later, at school, Tommy is bullied by Lonnie and two other classmates. Tommy wobbles along, carrying a large pumpkin, while Lonnie and two other boys, Richie (Mickey Yablans)[5] and Keith (Adam Hollander), taunt him. They make fun of his 'little pumpkin' and ask, 'How's the little witches?' When Tommy demands that they leave him alone, they chant 'He's gonna get you' which Lonnie punctuates by announcing 'The boogeyman is coming.' Lonnie asks, 'Don't you know what happens on Halloween?' Tommy, mustering up some courage, replies, 'Yeah, we get candy!' The bullies mock Tommy's apparent naiveté. When he attempts to escape, they trip him, and he falls on the pumpkin, smashing it and his innocent dreams of a Halloween full of candy and bereft of terror.

The scene reveals not only divisions and hostility among the preadolescent group, but also shows the complicated stages of belief and maturation in *Halloween*. The film does not present a binary of belief/disbelief in the supernatural that easily corresponds with innocence/experience. The bullying scene shows that there are many stages of maturation. There is the preadolescent like Tommy who believes in a kindly, magical Halloween— supernatural but not scary—bringing with it a bounty of candy. Next, there is the sinister stage of preadolescent belief inhabited by Lonnie and his accomplices. They make fun of Tommy not because he believes in the supernatural, but because he believes in its benevolence. Apparently, they know better, that the supernatural is a malevolent force to be feared. Their belief is confirmed later in the film when they show up at the Myers house. Even without a Tommy to bully, dissent among the preadolescent ranks still exists. Richie taunts Lonnie, daring him to enter the Myers house. Keith encourages him, but Lonnie is still hesitant. Loomis, who is hiding and waiting for Michael, shoos them away by whispering from the bushes, 'Hey Lonnie, get your ass away from there.' The three boys flee, as if they all believe in the danger of the spirit world. However, the exact relationship with the supernatural that accompanies their beliefs varies. Does Richie dare Lonnie to enter the Myers house because he is more afraid or less? These disagreements suggest a spectrum of belief in the supernatural that cannot be pinned down by one's age.

Ostensibly, teenagers are at a stage where they no longer believe in the supernatural—either benevolent or malevolent—but these positions on the spectrum of belief and disbelief in *Halloween* are not immutably fixed. Laurie seems to be the model of mature skepticism. When Tommy tells her that Richie said the boogeyman was coming for him, she rationally explains: 'Tommy, Halloween night is when people play tricks on each other. It's all make believe. I think Richie was just trying to scare you.' When Tommy remains uncertain, she assures him that, as the mature person in charge, she will take care of him if anything happens: 'The boogeyman can only come out on Halloween night, right? . . . Well, I'm here tonight. I'm not about to let anything happen to you.' However, Laurie's position as a rational disbeliever is not stable. Earlier in the film, when startled by noises that turn out to be preadolescent trick-or-treaters next door, Laurie wistfully chides herself, 'Well kiddo, I thought you outgrew superstition.' However, she is less wistful when he sees Michael in her backyard. She whispers to herself, 'Calm down. This is ridiculous,' as she lies down on a bed that looks too small for her, as if she is regressing in age. Laurie's fearful tremors demonstrate how a teen can regress into petrified preadolescence at a moment's notice. After her encounter with Michael, she regresses again. Like a terrified child, she sits on the floor, cries, and looks up at Loomis, meekly asking, 'Was that the boogeyman?' If Laurie regresses into preadolescence, Tommy attempts to move in the opposite direction. Bored by Laurie's reading of a King Arthur children's book, Tommy shows off his maturing taste in literature, displaying a stash of comic books hidden from his mother (see Figure 3.7). With no bullies around, Tommy becomes the tormentor as he tries to scare Lindsey by hiding behind a curtain and whispering her name and grabbing her from behind and threatening 'He's gonna getcha!' Like Laurie, however, Tommy returns to a state of child-like terror when he sees Michael outside. Tommy demonstrates the complicated, nonlinear process of growing up depicted in *Halloween*.

While Tommy undergoes a dynamic journey, oscillating between poles on the youth spectrum, Lindsey, his prepubescent counterpart, is relegated to a comparatively static position. If *Halloween* gives precedence to its female teenage characters over males, the opposite is true for its preadolescent characters. In this way, *Halloween* is typical of coming-of-age stories that focus on male experiences and their 'dominant connection to the public sphere' (Kearney 2002: 126). Tommy interacts with the public sphere through his relationship with his peers at school and grapples with

Figure 3.7 Tommy's maturing tastes

questions of fear and belief. Conversely, the film does not depict Lindsey's interactions with the public sphere, nor does it delve into her inner struggles. While Tommy talks with Laurie and asks questions, Lindsey sits silently frozen on the couch watching television, an occasional victim of Tommy's scare tactics. Like female characters from traditional coming-of-age stories, Lindsey is associated with the private, domestic sphere (126–127). These stories are also structured around the girl's 'involvement in romance' (127). In this vein, the most agency Lindsey exhibits in the film is when she makes the choice to pair with Tommy and support him. Annie's scheme to leave the Wallace house to pick up Paul only works because Lindsey jumps at the chance to watch television with Tommy. Her allegiance with Tommy is confirmed later when he attempts to scare her. He sneaks behind a curtain and whispers her name. As he is hiding, he sees Michael outside, backs away from the window, and bumps into Lindsey. They both scream, and Tommy hysterically yells, 'The boogeyman's outside!' Laurie rushes into the room, wraps her arms around Lindsey, and reprimands Tommy. He plops on the couch and whines, 'Nobody believes me.' Lindsey declares, 'I believe you, Tommy,' steps away from Laurie, and sits beside him. Lindsey seems to have already decided to be Tommy's unwavering partner.

Lindsey's devotion reflects the speed with which girls are expected to mature into women in traditional coming-of-age stories. Mary Celeste Kearney argues that 'the swift transformation of a girl into a woman' in these stories leads female characters from being dependent upon their parents to being dependent upon their husbands (126). Indeed, when Laurie later looks in on Tommy and Lindsey after she has put them to bed in the Doyles' master bedroom, they look like an old married couple. Earlier in the film, Bob makes a disturbing joke. Before he and Lynda storm into the Wallace house, Bob explains, 'First, I rip your clothes off . . . then you rip my clothes off, then we rip Lindsey's clothes off.' It is a throwaway joke—albeit a disturbing one about sexually assaulting a preadolescent—but it also reflects the pressure placed on girls to quickly become women so that they can support and edify their male partners. *Halloween*'s trio of teenagers reflects the pressure on women to grow up and support the family (Laurie) and satiate men's desires (Annie and Lynda). In Haddonfield, girls must mature quickly.

Extended Adolescence and Criminal Justice: Michael Myers as Young Adult

No other youth character in *Halloween* resists growing up as much as Michael. Readings of Michael as a child trapped in a man's body often connect Michael with Tommy. Wood argues that Michael projects himself into Tommy's preadolescent body when he first sees Tommy and Laurie when they stop at the Myers house. According to Wood, Michael views Laurie as 'the reincarnation of the sister he murdered as a child' because he sees her with Tommy, 'who resembles him as he was' when he murdered Judith (1979a: 26). Leeder agrees with this reading, calling Michael 'an over-grown, arrested child' who does not harm Tommy because he '[identifies] with him instead' (Leeder 2014: 79). But this equation has some problems. Laurie is an odd substitute for Judith given how dissimilar they are. Actually, after Michael's killing spree, Annie is the one he puts in Judith's place when he ceremoniously displays her dead body, lying on a bed with Judith's stolen tombstone resting above her head. After Tommy and Laurie split up, Michael does take Tommy's place by Laurie's side on her morning journey as he trails her to Haddonfield High and spies on her. However, Michael briefly interrupts his day-long surveillance of Laurie to make a detour to Tommy's school in a scene that suggests (through visual details, as is Carpenter's method) Michael is unable to completely identify with Tommy. After the bullies trip Tommy, causing him to smash his pumpkin, they run away. Richie exits through an entryway in a chain-link fence around the school. He cuts left and runs directly into Michael, the impact emphasized by a sting from Carpenter's score. Michael stops Richie by grabbing his shoulders. Shocked, Richie looks up at Michael, then turns and runs the other way. Michael does not pursue him but instead watches Tommy. In the background of the shot, a dejected Tommy abandons his smashed pumpkin and begins walking to the left. In the foreground, Michael walks alongside him, nearly parallel. It seems as if Tommy and Michael are in sync, which may suggest identification, but during the entire tracking shot, the chain-link fence stands between them, as if to suggest a barrier that Michael cannot cross (see Figure 3.8). Michael may want to identify with Tommy, but Michael's emerging adulthood keeps him from completely doing so.

Figure 3.8 Michael stalks Tommy

It may be more accurate to classify Michael as a 'young adult,' a youth category that has become more prominent in US culture during the past couple of decades. In early studies of youth cinema, 'youth' usually extends from ages 12 to 20 (Shary 2014: 19). However, the window widened in the 1990s, as several popular culture studies defined 'youth' as ranging from 12 to the mid-20s (23). Currently, the ceiling has risen even further. David Pimentel argues that various societal shifts have extended adolescence, as a majority of 'emerging adults remain in a dependent relationship with their parents well into their twenties' (Pimentel 2013: 82). In contemporary culture, 'Twenty-five is the new 18, and delayed adolescence is no longer a theory, but a reality' (Stetka 2017). While these attitudes were not prominent in 1978, looking at *Halloween* from this perspective throws into relief the image of Michael as a young adult driven by a violent desire to flee from the shackles of adulthood.

Considering Michael as a young adult rather than a man-child stuck in arrested development reveals possible motivations behind Michael's murderous behavior. Explanations of Michael's motives generally fall into one of two categories: Either Michael's actions are the result of festering psychological traumas engendered by sexual repression *vis-à-vis* the incest taboo, or Michael, as Loomis insists, is the embodiment of pure evil. Looking at Michael as a young adult—an individual whose age suggests he should be mature but whose behaviors are still given to youthful impulses—provides a third explanation in line with the film's depiction of the failure of social institutions. Perhaps the criminal justice system attempts to treat Michael as an adult before he is willing—or mentally able—to accept this responsibility. In retaliation, Michael defiantly acts like a cruel child. Pimental contends that juvenile justice institutions should take extended adolescence into account when sentencing young people to 'regain its focus on reclaiming and rehabilitating wayward kids' and abandon 'the highly retributive adult system that will only give up on their potential and lock them away for the bulk of their lives' (2013: 74). By neglecting to consider changes in cultural attitudes toward youth and forcing young adults to take accountability for wrongdoings that they may not fully understand—thus building up resentment rather than reform—a continuing reliance on the 'retributive adult system' creates more problems than it solves.

By not considering Michael's delayed adolescence, the criminal justice system creates a warped young adult stuck in a liminal space between childhood and maturity. Michael's reign of terror begins when his passage from childhood to adulthood is commemorated by his transportation to stand trial as an adult. The paradigm of the 'highly retributive' system of justice is at work. On the ride to pick up Michael, Loomis declares he 'never, never, never' wants Michael to be released from custody. Taking Michael to stand trial is a formality for him. Michael escapes, stealing the station wagon meant to transport him, and drives toward Haddonfield, just as a young adult may flee from the responsibilities of impending adulthood. Michael's ability to drive is one of the film's biggest mysteries. Wood calls it 'a bit of meaningless mystification' (1979a: 26), but there may be more to it. His ability to drive may symbolize that the juvenile justice system in which he was imprisoned taught him the ostensible skills of adulthood (like driving), but little else. After Michael's escape, Loomis complains to Dr. Wynn that they did not take the danger posed by Michael seriously enough. When Loomis insists that Michael is headed for Haddonfield, Wynn declares that is impossible because Michael is unable to drive. Loomis angrily yells, 'He was doing very well last night! Maybe someone around here gave him lessons.'

Loomis's sarcasm may reveal the deficiencies of a juvenile justice system that teaches its inmates nothing but the most hollow, rote, and mechanical aspects of being an adult—like learning to drive a car—and then turns them out when they reach an arbitrarily determined legal age. In the interim, the child's mind and body physically grow, but nothing is placed in the new spaces of the youth's consciousness. So these new spaces remain vacant, leaving the youth with only the flimsy appearance of adulthood. Michael's mask is the perfect metonymic signifier of his subjectivity. The shape of a human is there—for all of Loomis's talk of Michael being inhuman, Michael still picks a human mask, as opposed to a werewolf or other creature—but without the expression, feeling, and emotion a person typically learns in their youth.

The stolen sanitarium station wagon becomes a symbol of the institutionalization that took away Michael's youth and continues to imprison him. When the school day ends for Tommy, Michael first follows Tommy on foot, with the fence separating the imprisoned Michael from his childhood. Michael gets into the station wagon and slowly drives behind Tommy as he walks along the sidewalk. The automobile puts even more distance between Michael and Tommy. The scene is shot from the backseat of the station wagon behind a wire grid screen separating the front and backseat, so that Tommy appears behind the bars of the grid. Technically, Michael, sitting in the front seat behind the wheel, is on the same side of the bars as Tommy, but graphically, the image recalls the fence that separated them on foot and the bars that separated Michael from his youth. Michael pulls up beside Tommy, and for a moment, the camera's view is unobscured. However, Tommy never turns his head to notice, much less recognize, Michael. If Michael is seeking a look of recognition from Tommy, he does not receive it. When Tommy does finally see Michael, his reaction is one of horror, not identification. The only time that Laurie, Annie, and Lynda all see Michael is when he drives by and slows to a crawl in the station wagon. Due to the automotive signifier, Lynda and Annie both mistake Michael for a peer. Laurie suspects that the driver is someone who is both socially unequipped to deal with adolescent emotions and too old to be hitting on high school girls. Having missed out on his adolescence, Michael is thrust unprepared into young adulthood. He is the monster reincarnation of the juvenile delinquent of youth cinema's past.

Conclusion

This chapter argues that with its six youth characters—three teenagers, two preadolescents, and one young adult—*Halloween* addresses a wide spectrum of youth themes. While the three teenage main characters are not incredibly developed, analyzing them using Shary's taxonomy of character types in school films allows a fuller appreciation of how Carpenter and Hill economically craft their personas with just a few lines of dialogue and some subtle visual cues, like those during Laurie and Annie's conversation during their dusk-time commute. The preadolescent characters they watch over during babysitting duties add another layer to *Halloween*'s depiction of youth. This chapter maintains that the film uses its preadolescent characters to explore the complexities of emotional maturation and fear, finding that there is no straight line from childish belief in the supernatural to adult skepticism. Rather, *Halloween* finds characters oscillating between the two. Finally, the chapter contends that Michael is best understood not as an overgrown man-child, but instead as a young adult warped by an ineffective justice system that, rather than rehabilitating him, made him into a killing machine.

In exploring *Halloween*'s triptych of youth, this chapter demonstrates how Carpenter's film provides future slasher films with a rich cadre of character types from which to draw. Many teen slasher films draw from the sense of camaraderie between Laurie, Annie, and Lynda, while also imitating the type of divisions that arise amongst the teen group; Michael infiltrates the trio when two members of the group take advantage of the responsible one. In a similar fashion, other teenage groups in slasher films break apart based on issues of betrayal, jealousy, peer pressure, and/or irritation. From a plot perspective, these divisions come in handy, splitting up the group so the killer can pick them off.

Some youth character types featured in *Halloween* are typical of slasher films that followed, while others are less so. The presence of preadolescents in *Halloween* is atypical of films of the first slasher cycle. Preadolescent characters did not play a prominent role in any slasher films until *Friday the 13th: The Final Chapter* (Zito, 1984), released after the first slasher film cycle. The success of this film and *A Nightmare on Elm Street* a few months later kicked off a second slasher cycle (Nowell 2011: 249). The next two films in the *Friday* series—*Friday the 13th: A New Beginning* (Steinmann, 1985) and *Friday the 13th Part VI: Jason Lives* (McLoughlin, 1986)— would feature preadolescent characters, as would subsequent entries in the *Halloween* franchise like *Halloween 4: The Return of Michael Myers* (Little, 1988) and *Halloween 5: The Revenge of Michael Myers* (Othenin-Girard, 1989). More typical of slasher films that followed in the wake of *Halloween* is the mixed-up young adult who ends up being the masked killer. Both *Terror Train* and *My Bloody Valentine* feature this type of character. The hyperbolic *Sleepaway Camp* (Hiltzik, 1983), released months before the beginning of the second slasher cycle, combines the preadolescent character with the mixed-up killer to create one of the slasher subgenre's most bizarre climaxes. However, no future slasher films would so prominently meld together the preadolescent with the killer as director Rob Zombie's 2007 *Halloween* remake and its sequel two years later. Before arriving at this destination, the *Halloween* franchise's depiction of youth is an intriguing journey, coalescing with some trends and departing from others. The next chapter examines the *Halloween* franchise and its evolving depictions of youth.

Notes

1 While Nick Castle plays Michael for a majority of the film with production designer/editor Tommy Lee Wallace handling many of the inserts, Tony Moran provided a face for 21-year-old Michael when Laurie rips off his mask.
2 According to Carpenter (Anchor Bay 2013b), Debra Hill directed this scene.
3 In 1981, Carpenter shot additional scenes to use in *Halloween*'s network broadcast debut. One of these scenes reveals that Lynda borrowed the blouse from Laurie.
4 This scene contains what is perhaps the most iconic nuance of Castle's performance as Michael. After pinning Bob to the wall, Michael pauses for a moment to look at him. Michael tilts his head back and forth, as if admiring his handiwork. In 2018's *Halloween*, Castle retuned to perform this head tilt in one scene.
5 Son of producer Irwin Yablans.

4 The *Mise en Abyme* of Youth

The *Halloween* Franchise

When Loomis finds that Michael's body has disappeared after falling from the second story of the Doyle house, the film ends with a sequence of shots of the domestic spaces Michael has infiltrated. As the film presents a series of tableaus from the Doyle and Wallace households—the rooms and staircases now eerily vacant—the sound of Michael's heavy breathing pulsates on the soundtrack, increasing in volume over Carpenter's manic theme. The sequence concludes with a shot of the Myers house and then cuts to black. It is a spectacular ending, rich with connotation. The ending is also dynamite from a commercial perspective. *Halloween* has what Carolyn Jess-Cooke calls 'sequel logic,' that is, a film containing 'the possibility of a sequel within the primary narrative' (2009: 10). While Carpenter had no intention of making a sequel, *Halloween*'s franchise potential was infinite, and after the sleeper success of the film, a sequel was inevitable. During this time, sequels were becoming more prevalent, especially among horror films; the summer of 1978 saw the release of *Jaws 2* (Szwarc, 1978) and *Damien: The Omen II* (Taylor and Hodges, 1978). *Halloween* financiers Yablans and Akkad were set to make a sequel 'with or without' his and Hill's participation, so he and Hill decided to oversee the production of the sequel (Anchor Bay 2013a). The result, 1981's *Halloween II*, was followed immediately by *Halloween III: Season of the Witch* (Wallace, 1982), an attempt to reimagine the franchise as an anthology series. The film bombed and was followed by five more sequels, a remake, the remake's sequel, and finally, in 2018, a film that acted as a direct sequel to the first film, ignoring all other entries. All told, there are 11 entries in the *Halloween* franchise.

This chapter offers an overview of the sequels and remakes of the *Halloween* franchise, arguing that the franchise has, with a few exceptions, adapted to youth horror trends. *Halloween* films generally fare well when box office conditions are favorable for youth horror, but the franchise often cannot overcome an adverse market. This chapter argues that, regardless of box office, the franchise's depiction of youth characters has evolved over the past few decades and resulted in some surprising representations of youth in slasher cinema, with perhaps the most unique being the prominent roles played by preadolescents in later films, something foreshadowed by the role of preadolescents in the first film. This chapter concludes that the *Halloween* films create a *mise en abyme* of youth, an infinitely recurring cycle of young characters to keep the franchise alive for generations.

Xerox and Anti-Xerox: *Halloween II* and *Halloween III*

Carpenter and Hill went to great lengths to tie the sequel to the original: They wrote the screenplay and produced; Curtis and Pleasence revisited their leading roles; and Dean Cundy, the first film's cinematographer, returned to maintain the original's palette and lighting design. The main personnel change was a new director, Rick Rosenthal. Carpenter and Hill decided to have the film begin immediately after the conclusion of the first film and sought to seamlessly suture the sequel to the original. However, the union is not entirely seamless, as there are elements that differentiate the two films, one of which is the deemphasis of youth characters. The majority of the film takes place at Haddonfield Memorial Hospital, where Laurie is taken for care after the events of the first film. Michael (Dick Warlock) randomly murders a teenager (Anne Bruner) on his way to the hospital to kill Laurie. The film reveals that Laurie is Michael's sister, and this is the reason he targeted her. However, Laurie is catatonic for most of the film, lying in a hospital bed. The film's victim group is mainly made up of hospital employees like Mrs. Alves (Gloria Gifford), the night shift manager, and Janet (Ana Alicia), a buttoned-down nurse. While a couple of characters like Jill (Tawney Moyer), a nurse, and Jimmy (Lance Guest), an ambulance driver, are close to Laurie's age, the rest of the hospital staff have adult demeanors. Rather than chatting about boys, school, and other teenage topics, these characters are stressed about getting to work on time. At the time, teen slasher films were seeing rapidly diminishing returns at the box office, while other types of horror films continued to perform well (Nowell 2011: 230–231), which may explain why Carpenter and Hill recalibrated their approach, deemphasizing youth and making *Halloween II* feel like a horror film but not a teen slasher.[1] *Halloween II* was a hit and firmly established the brand. However, Carpenter later revealed that working on the film was a chore for him and bemoaned that the writing process felt like 'Xeroxing' (Anchor Bay 2013a). Carpenter and Hill drastically veered away from Xeroxing with the next film in the franchise, *Halloween III: Season of the Witch*, which he would co-produce with Hill (while also doing some uncredited rewrites and co-scoring the film with Alan Howarth). If *Halloween II* was a Xerox, *III* would be an anti-Xerox.

Carpenter and Hill attempted to redefine the franchise with *Halloween III*, but the rebranding failed. Growing tired of the slasher film narrative (and no doubt noting that slasher films were dying at the box office), Carpenter and Hill jettisoned the scenario of Michael Myers stalking victims in Haddonfield and instead sought to transform the franchise into an anthology series with each film based around the Halloween holiday (Carlomagno 1982: 8). Wallace's film tells the bizarre story of a doctor (Tom Atkins) and the daughter of one of his deceased patients (Stacey Nelkin) who find themselves in the middle of a plot by toy company owner Conal Cochran (Dan O'Herlihy), who manufactures incredibly popular, faddish Halloween masks. Cochran's mysterious corporation plans to broadcast a signal via a watch-and-win commercial on Halloween night that will kill every child wearing the trendy mask, causing their heads to melt into a mess of snakes and insects. The outlandish film failed to connect with audiences, especially those expecting a new installment of the story of Michael Myers.

Eschewing the previous films' logo and color scheme, *Halloween III*'s poster features a red demonic face hovering above three preadolescent children, an apt image since the only youth characters in the film are anonymous preadolescents who are potential fodder for the toymaker's master plan. With no teenagers around, the only preadolescent character with any depth is Buddy (Bradley Schacter), a spoiled brat who offers the toymaker—in a manner reminiscent of a Bond villain—an opportunity to demonstrate the lethality of his deadly masks to the captured protagonists. Despite *Halloween III*'s quirky, B-movie charm, the film's $14.4 million US gross was a disappointment compared with the first two films. Carpenter and Hill had a hit with *Halloween II*, which featured more mature characters than the original film, but the failure of *Halloween III* suggested it was unwise to do away with teenagers altogether, not to mention ditching the brand identity. While the popularity and profitability of teen slashers had dwindled by late 1982, the third entry in Paramount's decidedly on-brand *Friday the 13th* series was a hit, perhaps suggesting that another slasher-style *Halloween* could have been a hit. Instead, an off-brand film derailed the *Halloween* series, and the franchise lay dormant throughout the mid-1980s.

'A Distasteful Display of Cinematic Child Abuse': *Return*, *Revenge*, and *Curse*

Beginning in 1984, the second slasher cycle was in full swing when, in 1986, 89 horror films went into production, a number that grew to 93 in 1987 (Kendrick 2014: 311). In 1986, mini-major Cannon Films approached Carpenter about making a fourth *Halloween* film. Carpenter and Hill still owned rights to the franchise, along with Moustapha Akkad, who took over

Yablans's share after the release of *Halloween III* when their partnership ended and they divided the assets (Yablans 2012: 199). Carpenter and Hill commissioned a screenplay from Dennis Etchison, who brought back the franchise's focus on teens as his story centered around Tommy and Lindsey from the first film, now teenagers (Assip 2017). After Akkad rejected Etchison's script, Carpenter and Hill sold their portion of the franchise to Akkad, whose company Trancas International now held sole stewardship of the series. Trancas produced *Halloween 4: The Return of Michael Myers* and released it on 21 October 1988. The ten-year anniversary of the original figured prominently in both the film's story and its marketing, with a poster that featured the classic *Halloween* logo and prominently featured the pale visage of Michael's mask, which was now the most recognizable signifier of the franchise.

Oddly enough, *Halloween 4* features a small teenage victim group. There are only three teens in the film's cast: Rachel Carruthers (Ellie Cornell), her romantic interest Brady (Sasha Jenson), and Kelly (Kathleen Kinmont), who has romantic designs on Brady. Kelly swoops in for a tryst with Brady when Rachel has to cancel a Halloween night date with him in order to watch Jamie (Danielle Harris), her 8-year-old adopted sister. Jamie is Laurie Strode's daughter, orphaned after her mother died in an automobile accident and recently adopted by the Carruthers. When Michael (George P. Wilbur) arrives in Haddonfield, he sets his sights on his niece Jamie, making her the focal point of the film. The narrative is built around a series of cat-and-mouse chases as Jamie is pursued by Michael and protected by Rachel and Loomis (again played by Donald Pleasence). As such, the teenage romantic triangle between Rachel, Brady, and Kelly is subordinated to Loomis's mission to capture Michael and Michael's obsessive quest to murder Jamie. One could argue that *Halloween 4* is not a dramatic departure from the slasher formula and that Rachel comfortably fits the Final Girl mold, but Rachel is rarely, if ever, the sole focus of the audience's empathy. Among the film's various chases of the film's final act, Jamie is the constant. She even has the ambiguously gendered name that Clover argues is characteristic of Final Girls (2015: 88).

It is possible to see the relatively significant role that preadolescents played in the original *Halloween* foreshadowing the emergence of Jamie, a preadolescent, as a prominent character in the franchise. If, as Yablans had argued during the height of the first teen slasher cycle, preadolescents made up a large contingent of the slasher film audience, his claim would be even more true during the late 1980s, when home video gave youth audiences under 17 years old easier access to films 'with no ratings restrictions' (Shary 2005: 56; Rockoff 2002: 2). Sue Short connects the stalking of younger victims in slashers to anxieties of the possible effects these films may have on preteens in the video era (2007: 57). For whatever reason, Trancas chose to emphasize Jamie as they moved forward with the franchise.

Halloween 4 rode the wave of the second slasher cycle to $17.7 million in US box office, a huge hit by Trancas' standards. Trancas immediately began production on *Halloween 5: The Revenge of Michael Myers* with a story that centered mostly around Jamie. The film's opening finds her residing at a children's hospital where she is recovering from the trauma caused by the events of the previous film, which have struck her mute. Rachel returns but is killed off 20 minutes into the film. Between scenes of Jamie being frightened by horrific visions due to a psychic link she now shares with him and hounded by Loomis who is seeking to use her to catch Michael, the audience is introduced to a quartet of teenagers whose deaths at Michael's hands seem perfunctory. One character, Mikey (Jonathan Chapin), is killed off after only one scene. Out of the group, Rachel's friend Tina (Wendy Kaplan), is the only one given any development, but she falls prey to Michael's knife before the final act. The film's climax takes place in the old Myers house, as Loomis and the police set up a sting operation to capture Michael. They use Jamie as bait, strategically placing her in an upstairs window. Predictably, things do not go as planned, and after Michael takes out Loomis and a police officer, Jamie must fend for herself, becoming the Final Girl who outsmarts Michael and survives long enough to be saved by a revived Loomis.

Halloween 5 was not the first slasher film to feature a preadolescent character in a substantial role—a 12-year-old (Corey Feldman) squared off with Jason in *Friday the 13th: The Final Chapter*—but the decision to feature a preadolescent character as a main character and the Final Girl may have been too much for some audiences. Even *Fangoria* was turned off by the film, with one reviewer describing Michael's attacks on Jamie as 'a distasteful display of cinematic child abuse' ('*Halloween 5*' 1990: 37). For whatever reason, the film failed to connect with audiences and would end up becoming the lowest grossing film of the *Halloween* franchise with $11.6 million in US box office, a letdown after the previous film's $17.7 million domestic take. *Halloween 4* was able to catch the wave as the second slasher cycle peaked in 1988, but in 1989, franchise fatigue plagued youth horror cinema. That summer, Paramount and New Line released the lowest grossing entries in, respectively, the *Friday the 13th* and *Nightmare on Elm Street* franchises. The novelty of a preadolescent protagonist was unable to lift the *Halloween* franchise out of the morass of a stagnant market. *Halloween 5* ended on a cliffhanger, but the fates of Michael and Jamie would have to wait for a stronger youth horror market to sustain them.

The market for youth horror was not much better six years later when *Halloween: The Curse of Michael Myers* (Chappelle, 1995), was released. The theatrical market for youth horror was at a low point,[2] and *Curse* seems to be flailing around, looking for direction. The making of the film, from script stage to post-production, was arduous and wracked with disagreements between Trancas and Bob and Harvey Weinstein, who had purchased partial ownership of the franchise and planned to distribute the film through Dimension Films, the genre label of Miramax Films.[3] The behind-the-scenes struggles are reflected in the film's odd premise. Jamie is captured by a druidic cult that gives Michael his supernatural ability to overcome death. Six years later, the cult impregnates Jamie (J.C. Brandy), who gives birth to a baby boy. Jamie escapes with the baby, and Michael pursues her, eventually catching and killing her. Michael intends to return the baby to the cult, but Jamie successfully hides the baby from him before she is killed. The infant is found by Tommy Doyle (Paul Rudd), the young boy whom Laurie Strode was babysitting in the first film. Now in his early 20s, Tommy has become obsessed with researching Michael and his possible motivations. He lives in a boarding house across the street from the old Myers house, which is currently inhabited by John Strode (Bradford English), the brother of Laurie Strode's adoptive father, and his family. John is abusive toward the family, especially his daughter, Kara (Marianne Hagan), who is in her mid-20s and has a young son, Danny (Devin Gardner), both of whom recently moved in with John and the family. Tommy keeps his eye on Kara and Danny from afar, suspecting that Michael will one day return for them since the cult's ancient rituals require that Michael sacrifice all of his relatives. After Tommy rescues Jamie's infant son, he knows that Michael will soon follow and approaches Kara and Danny, hoping to keep them safe. Michael and the cult eventually kidnap Kara, Danny, and the infant and take them back to their stronghold at Smith's Grove Sanitarium, leaving Tommy to team up with Loomis to rescue them.

Michael's victim group in *Curse* ranges from the middle-aged (Kara's parents) to young adult (an offensive radio shock-jock looking to broadcast live from the Myers house on Halloween night) to college age (Kara's brother and his girlfriend) and younger (Jamie), and the core victim group is made up of a range of youths. As a college-aged young mother, Kara makes for an odd Final Girl, perhaps further solidifying Nowell's point that the character type is actually not that prevalent. The male characters make up a *mise en abyme* of youth characters. In his mid-20s and still obsessed with Michael to the point of living across the street from the Myers house, Tommy is a man-child, and his preadolescence is reflected in Danny, who is the same age as Tommy was when he was first threatened by Michael. Further still, there is Stephen, the infant boy, who may represent the infinite regeneration and recycling of youth victims in *Halloween* films and, perhaps, the slasher film in general. An early scene shows the infant during a ritual, shot from a bird's eye angle. As the camera hovers over the scene and cranes in, the naked infant lies on an altar as a druid ceremoniously draws the cult's runic symbol in blood upon the baby's chest, a composition that gives the viewer a queasy sense of circularity. Tommy's voice-over ominously assures the viewer that evil never dies but merely rests a while before returning, as if the film is aware that its scenarios have been played out many times before. *Curse* could not overcome youth horror's dry spell and underperformed at the US box office with a $15.1 million gross, but its self-awareness prefigures the next direction that the teen slasher would take, a direction that would benefit the *Halloween* franchise.

Teenage Soap Horror: *H20* and *Resurrection*

Although *Curse* was a miss for Dimension when it debuted in October 1995, the studio would score with another slasher film just over a year later with the release of *Scream* (Craven, 1996) in December 1996. Grossing over $100 million in the US, *Scream* was the first hit teen slasher film in almost a decade. *Scream* was novel to audiences at the time because of its self-awareness, with characters who comment on the conventions of the story in which they exist. As Andrew Tudor notes, while *Scream* 'did not introduce self-consciousness about genre convention' into horror cinema, the film was the first 'highly commercial (and therefore influential)' horror film to fore-ground this type of 'knowing reflexivity' (2002: 110). Tudor also observes that *Scream*'s 'self-consciousness is contained: an occasion for humour and joyous audience involvement, but not a mechanism for questioning the workings of the horror movie as such' (*ibid.*). In other words, *Scream* never becomes parodic, and its references to past horror and slasher films pro-vide comedic relief or accentuate moments of suspense. During one scene, Randy (Jamie Kennedy), a horror movie buff, watches a slasher film on television. As the killer sneaks up behind the victim on screen, Randy yells at the television, imploring the victim to turn around, and fails to realize that a killer is sneaking up behind him.

Scream's screenplay, written by Kevin Williamson, was bolstered by a cast of hot young superstars, including Drew Barrymore, Neve Campbell from the television series *Party of Five* (1994–2000), and Courteney Cox from the show *Friends* (1994–2004). In the wake of *Scream*'s success fol-lowed a flood of teen slasher films featuring young television stars and glossy production values. During this time, Trancas was developing a direct-to-video *Halloween* sequel.[4] However, the Weinsteins, no doubt inspired by the success of *Scream* and its follow-ups, decided to make a high-profile *Halloween* sequel that would meld the post-*Scream* teen slasher film with *Halloween*'s status as the ur-text of the teen slasher (after all, *Halloween* is the film Randy is watching on television in *Scream*).

The result, *Halloween H20:20 Years Later* (Miner, 1998), is a film that is unique among post-*Scream* teen slasher films, while also being typical of the trend. Out of the multitude of teen slashers that followed *Scream* in the late 1990s, *H20* is the only sequel to a previously established slasher franchise, evidence of the franchise's ability to adapt to trends in youth horror. The film's sequel status is foundational to its premise. Dimension wanted to capitalize on the franchise's legacy by emphasizing that the release of *H20* coincided with the 20-year anniversary of the original film's release. The film also recalled the original by bringing back Jamie Lee Curtis to reprise the role of Laurie Strode, who had last appeared in *Halloween II*. *H20* creates a new continuity that ignores the events of the fourth, fifth, and sixth film, which were predicated on the idea that Laurie had died in an automobile accident. Instead, *H20* finds Laurie as the headmistress of a California boarding school, living under the name Keri Tate. She is divorced, has a son, John (Josh Hartnett), and has turned to alcohol to stave off the PTSD she suffers as a result of Michael's attack on her 20 years before.

H20 fits in comfortably with films that Peter Hutchings argues were marketed as 'being like *Scream*,' but only superficially resembling *Scream* and rarely including the copious 'knowing references to old horror films' to the extent that *Scream* does (2013: 212). This is the case with *H20*: Outside of references to previous *Halloween* films (which should be expected from a sequel), the film is only peppered with minor nods to films like *Psycho* (Janet Leigh appears in a cameo that recalls her role as Marion) and the *Friday the 13th* films (in one jump scare, a character pops up wearing a hockey mask). For the most part, the film resembles other teen horror films of its time, which Hutchings describes as 'teenage soap horror' (215). The two teen leads are young actors being groomed for stardom. Male lead Josh Hartnett was also filming *The Faculty* (Rodriguez, 1998), another teen horror film under production with Dimension, while making *H20*. Michelle Williams, who plays Molly, Hartnett's love interest, was also a lead actor on *Dawson's Creek* (1998–2003), a hit youth television show, created by *Scream* screenwriter Kevin Williamson, that premiered six months before *H20*'s release (see Figure 4.1).

Perhaps to demonstrate the acting chops of up-and-coming stars, teenage soap horror offers 'more developed characterisations' than slasher films of the past (Hutchings 2013: 216), which is the case with *H20*. The film fleshes out the strained relationship between Keri and John, as Keri's fear of Michael's return has led to her being overbearing and John chafing under her protectiveness. Besides John and Molly, the film features only two other teen characters, another couple (Adam Hann-Byrd and Jodi Lyn O'Keefe) who are friends with John and Molly. Fewer characters allow for 'greater focus on the interpersonal dynamics' of the youth group, which Hutchings

Figure 4.1 'Teenage soap horror': *Halloween H20*

cites as a hallmark of teenage soap horror (214). All three members of John's teenage cohort are invested in his rebellion against his mother's restrictions, a connection to the main plot of Keri's confrontation with her greatest fear—Michael's return—that keeps the teen characters from getting lost in the shuffle like they do in *Halloween 5*'s overly busy plot. Keri's fear of Michael's return and for John's life directly relates to another characteristic Hutchings notes in teenage soap horror: the need for alertness. These films feature characters who must 'probe into the past . . . to make sense of the present and then to be able to act decisively' (215). Accordingly, Keri stresses that John be vigilant in case Michael returns. John does not heed her warning, and even though he survives when Michael invades a Halloween sleepover he and his friends have at the school, it is chance, not strategy, that allows him to survive until Keri arrives to save him and Molly. Hutchings notes that with the focus on intergroup dynamics and more developed characters, the role of the Final Girl is diminished in teenage soap horror. However, this is not the case in *H20*, as long as one can consider, as Short does, Keri as one of a group of grown-up Final Girls in late '90s cinema who must continue to take steps toward full maturity even after they have children of their own (Short 2007: 58–60). The film and its characters fit comfortably in the 'teenage soap' cycle, and *H20* grossed $55 million in box office, becoming the highest grossing film of the *Halloween* series, second only to the original when adjusted for inflation.

The success of *H20* guaranteed a follow-up, and with the next film in the series, *Halloween: Resurrection* (Rosenthal, 2002), the franchise adopted another mode that had proven successful for at least one horror film: found footage. The sleeper success of the low-budget found footage film *The Blair*

Witch Project (Sanchez and Myrick, 1999) was a media sensation, but as Rick Worland notes, the 'reality-based' style of the film was 'less related to the horror film' and more in tune with reality-based television programming of the time (2007: 114). *Halloween: Resurrection* was the first high-profile horror film to adopt the found footage mode and nested it within a narrative that also connected the film to the reality-based entertainment craze of the early 2000s and the rise of the Internet. In the film, reality show entrepreneur Freddie Harris (Busta Rhymes) launches a web series titled *Dangertainment*. He recruits a group of six college students, equipped with webcams, to spend a night in the Myers house, exploring the ruined house to discover Michael's motivation for killing (with phony evidence planted by Freddie). Unfortunately, Michael shows up and begins picking off the contestants. *Resurrection*'s premise plays off of the 'game' aspect that Vera Dika (1990) argues is integral to the slasher film, while also demonstrating the importance of being 'aware of the rules of the game' that Hutchings notes in teenage soap horror (2013: 216). The film shoehorns in a smorgasbord of youth trends—Brennan Klein describes the film as 'a top-to-bottom exercise in attempting to rip from the headlines of *TigerBeat* magazine' (Klein 2018)—but the film could not transcend declining interest in youth horror, which, by this point, was being parodied by the *Scary Movie* franchise (2000–2013). Again, the franchise moved with the trend, and *Resurrection*'s box office take dropped $25 million from *H20*'s in the US.

Return to Preadolescence: Rob Zombie's *Halloween* and *Halloween II*

In October 2003, the box office success of *The Texas Chainsaw Massacre* remake (Nispel, 2003) set off a trend of remakes of high-profile horror titles.[5] Trancas and The Weinstein Company (the Weinsteins took Dimension with them when they departed Miramax) revisited the *Halloween* franchise, recruiting heavy metal musician-turned-director Rob Zombie to write and direct a film that could 'reboot' the series, that is, give the franchise a fresh start and establish ground for future installments (Proctor 2012: 4–5). Zombie's *Halloween* (2007) would end up being 'perhaps the most notorious, polarizing horror remake' of the time (Nelson 2010: 120). Zombie made dramatic changes to the *Halloween* mythos, many of which related to the film's depiction of youth, more specifically, the revised origin of Michael Myers.

Michael's youth is pushed to the foreground in Zombie's version, a depiction some argue is ideologically potent. The original film elides Michael's childhood, only suggesting that Michael hails from a suburban middle class background, but Zombie spends significant amount of time exploring

Figure 4.2 Michael Myers: Abandoned child

Michael's youth, beginning when Michael (Daeg Faerch) is 10 years old (see Figure 4.2). As discussed in Chapter 2, Robin Wood was frustrated by the original film, arguing that it suggests Michael is an embodiment of 'pure evil' and neglects to develop the possibility that Michael is a construct of his socioeconomic position in the capitalist patriarchy. However, Andrew Patrick Nelson argues that the type of criticism offered by Wood is 'explicitly built into' Zombie's remake (2010: 129). According to Nelson, Michael's 'traumatic childhood [back-story]' in Zombie's film is 'so apparent' that it makes 'the application of any psychoanalytic theory redundant' (*ibid.*). In other words, everything Wood is looking for in the original—the ultimate family horror film, the violent release of repressed sexuality—is abundant in the remake. David Roche agrees, writing that *Halloween* is 'the most political' horror remake of the 2000s and is tantamount to an academic essay that 'follow[s] Robin Wood's advice' and 'read[s] the whole film against [Dr. Loomis]' (2014: 35, 46).

Zombie goes about this reading by offering an extended look at Michael's childhood. Zombie's previous films featured killers and murderers who come from underclass, 'white trash' environments (Bernard 2014: 123–132). Zombie's Michael is a product of this type of beleaguered background. He is abused by his stepfather (William Forsythe), ignored by his sister (Hanna Hall), and bullied at school. He seems to have a nurturing relationship with his mother (Sherri Moon Zombie), but she is too overwhelmed with work (as an exotic dancer) and other responsibilities to spend much time with him. The film's narrative 'strongly insists on the environmental and familial factors that seem to have come into play' when Michael explodes and murders a school bully (Daryl Sabara), his stepfather, his sister, and her boyfriend (Adam Weisman) (Roche 2014: 47). After Michael is institution-alized, Dr. Loomis (Malcolm McDowell) works with him, trying to make what seems like a genuine connection. However, his efforts are undermined by his tendency to diagnose and catalog Michael's condition in a sensation-alistic manner, which recalls the institutional failure depicted in the original film. Michael continues to emotionally retreat, eventually refusing to speak, and murders a nurse (Sybil Danning). Distraught and defeated, Michael's mother commits suicide, and Loomis gives up on Michael and monetizes their relationship by writing a lurid book about him. When grown-up Michael (Tyler Mane) escapes, Loomis follows and catches up with him as he is about to murder Laurie (Scout Taylor-Compton), his younger sister. Loomis begs him to let her go, pleading, 'Look, it's not her fault. Michael, it's my fault. I failed you.' Loomis's admission, coupled with the film's con-clusion, which returns to Michael's childhood via 8mm home movies inter-spersed through the closing credits, reinforce the notion that institutional failure and preadolescent trauma combine to create a monster like Michael. As such, Zombie's films replies to both Tudor's and Wood's readings of the film. The image of the preadolescent in the *Halloween* franchise travels along a peculiar trajectory, from bystanders like Tommy in the original film, to preadolescent Final Girl Jamie in the fifth, to murderer in Zombie's film.

Teenage characters also play an important role in Zombie's depictions of youth in his ideological transformation of the *Halloween* story. If Car-penter disavowed the possibility that Michael could be the product of Had-donfield, Zombie makes it clear how Haddonfield could create Michael. Zombie gives the main trio of girls—Laurie, Annie (Danielle Harris),[6] and Lynda (Kristina Klebe)—savage 'mean girl' makeovers that convey Had-donfield's abrasiveness. The difference between the original Lynda and Zombie's Lynda offers an example. Unlike the 'popular girl' of the original film, Lynda does not care about maintaining appearances, like learning new cheers or getting her hair done. During cheerleading practice, she jokes that the squad should 'rock it commando' and 'flash some snatch' for the audi-ence rather than learn a new cheer and is angry when the coach—whom she refers to as a 'dried up fuckin' bitch'—contacts her father.[7] Beyond giving her father the 'Miss sweetie-pants princess suck-up routine' to keep out of trouble, Lynda does not seem inclined to put up a performance for anyone else, including her boyfriend (Nick Mennell) with whom she is brutally hon-est about his lack of sexual prowess. Annie (Danielle Harris), once the rebel, is now aligned with authority, as represented by her father (Brad Dourif). On their walk home from school, Laurie, Annie, and Lynda see Michael watching them from across the street. Instead of throwing sarcastic barbs, Annie threatens him with the law: 'Hey asshole, my daddy's the sheriff! Why don't you crawl back under your fucking rock?' Haddonfield's youth are no longer united against authority but now collude with it to threaten those who have been ostracized by social institutions. Finally, Laurie is far from the classic 'nerd,' obsessed with academics and hesitant to engage in relationships. Her academics are never mentioned, and when Annie tries to set her up with Ben Tramer, she is not horrified but excited by the prospect.

Laurie is also no longer the nurturing babysitter, a sign that young people no longer look out for each other in Zombie's Haddonfield. When Tommy Doyle (Skyler Gisondo) spots her on her walk to school, she groans, 'Oh god, leave me alone, Tommy.' When he later confides in Laurie about his fear of the boogeyman, Laurie does not give him a motherly talk but instead makes fun of him. In the original film, death is able to infiltrate the youth group only after betrayal breaks the group apart, a dissolution that begins with Annie blackmailing Laurie. In Zombie's *Halloween*, however, betrayal and hostility are present from the beginning, before Halloween night begins. In her first scene, Annie badgers Laurie into taking care of Lindsey so she can hook up with Paul, and she later calls Lynda a 'slut.' Lynda reveals to Laurie later on the phone that Annie hurt her feelings. Lynda says, 'I don't give a shit about what Annie thinks anyway,' suggesting that there has been tension between the two for a while. Before hanging up, Lynda tells Laurie that she cares what Laurie thinks about her, but this exchange reveals the rifts that already exist in their circle. If Carpenter's Haddonfield was an environment in which youths are failed and abandoned by social institutions, Zombie's Haddonfield is a place where young people fail and abandon each other.

Despite the mixed reaction to Zombie's *Halloween*, the film performed well at the box office with a $58.2 million gross, leading to a sequel, written and directed by Zombie and released in 2009. With *Halloween II*, Zombie continues his bleak, critical autopsy of Haddonfield, digging deeper into themes introduced in the first film. Loomis is now an opportunistic media personality shamelessly promoting yet another book about Michael. The boundaries between 'normality/Haddonfield' and 'the Monster/Michael' erode as Laurie has a psychological breakdown. She suffers from PTSD after the events of the previous film and lives with Sheriff Brackett and Annie, who, like Laurie, barely survived Michael's attack and is dealing with the residual trauma. Laurie makes a couple of new young friends (Brea Grant and Angela Trimbur), but their friendship is not developed as much as Laurie's psychological struggle and tragically deteriorating relationship with Annie. Laurie has hallucinations about Michael and his mother, and her psychological recovery is derailed when she learns from Loomis's new book that she is Michael's biological sister and was adopted by the Strodes as an infant. Meanwhile, Michael escapes from the authorities after the events of the first film and hides out in the woods. He has visions of his mother as well and, conjuring an image of himself in preadolescence, communicates with her. He waits until Halloween to wreak bloody vengeance upon Haddonfield. This time around, Annie and Loomis do not survive their encounters with him. Laurie goes insane and is institutionalized. Haddonfield, with its savage values masquerading behind a bourgeois veneer, has created another monster. The film is relentlessly bleak, which may explain its disappointing box office performance. For the first time, the *Halloween* franchise's financial performance diverged from the trend. Usually, the performance of *Halloween* films tracked with comparable titles. However, in 2009, high-profile horror remakes like *My Bloody Valentine 3-D* (Lussier, 2009) and *Friday the 13th* (Nispel, 2009) did healthy business,[8] but *Halloween II* brought in $33.3 million, a little over half the gross of the previous film. While *Halloween II*'s underwhelming business could be attributed to several factors, the film's unrelenting atmosphere and dark depiction of youth did not help.

The Night Carpenter Came Home

Halloween fans celebrated when it was announced in May 2016 that John Carpenter was returning to the franchise. As an executive producer, he would work with Trancas, Miramax (Dimension lost rights to the property in 2016 [Miska 2015]), and Blumhouse Productions and would help choose the screenplay and director. The pitch that ultimately won out was from an unlikely team; writer/director David Gordon Green, who had directed mostly comedies and low-budget dramas, and writing partners, Danny McBride, best known as a comedic actor, and Jeff Fradley scored the gig. It was Jason Blum of Blumhouse Productions who approached Green about submitting a pitch (Artz 2017). Blum had proven to have a keen commercial sense; specializing in low-budget horror, Blumhouse had delivered a string of commercial and critical hits over the past decade, from *Paranormal Activity* (Peli, 2009) to *Get Out* (Peele, 2017). His solicitation of Green's pitch turned out to be another profitable enterprise, as Green and company's pitch evolved into a hit film that would end up being the top grossing film of the franchise and the highest grossing slasher film ever (Sprague 2018). While the original film was still more profitable in adjusted dollars, Green's film came close.

Green's *Halloween* ignored all other sequels and picked up the storyline 40 years after the events of the original film. Curtis returned to play Laurie. This iteration of the character is not Michael's sister but a random victim of his attack 40 years ago. Laurie's experience drove her into becoming a reclusive survivalist, residing in a fenced-in compound, complete with surveillance cameras and an arsenal of firearms. Michael (James Jude Courtney) has been incarcerated for the past 40 years. Laurie's paranoia about his possible escape has ruined two marriages and estranged her from her adult daughter, Karen (Judy Greer), who, in turn, keeps her teenage daughter, Allyson (Andi Matichak), from having a relationship with Laurie. When Michael escapes during a prison transfer, Laurie's fears are realized. Michael murders his way through Haddonfield and finds Allyson. The conclusion of the film finds Laurie, Karen, and Allyson at Laurie's compound in a final showdown with Michael, with the three women emerging triumphant. They lure Michael into a trap designed by Laurie and set the house on fire, leaving Michael to burn alive. The final shot of the film shows the women riding away from the burning house in the bed of a pickup truck. Laurie rests her head on Karen's shoulder to the left and locks arms on the right with Allyson. All three women hold bloody hands that rest in Laurie's lap.

The success of 2018's *Halloween* seemingly places it far away from the financial and critical disappointment of 1995's *Halloween: The Curse of Michael Myers* on the franchise's spectrum, but comparing the two films offers insight into the franchise's relationship with the larger youth horror cinema marketplace. Both films demonstrate how the *Halloween* franchise, for the most part, moves with larger market trends. The youth horror market was stagnant and directionless at the time of *Curse*'s release in 1995, a lack of direction evident in the film's convoluted story. In 2018, the market for youth horror was holding steady, accounting for around ten of the year's top 100 grossing films. 2018's *Halloween* no doubt benefited from this interest in youth horror, but it likely benefited even more from audiences' interest in familiar titles and properties. In 2018, sequels, spin-offs, remakes, and adaptations of pre-existing media properties made up 16 of the year's top 20 grossing films. 2018's *Halloween*, with its nebulous status as sequel, remake, and/or reboot, was perfect for this market and was the 21st highest grossing film of the year in the US with $159 million. By comparison, in 1995, only six of the year's top 20 films were sequels; *Curse* clocked in at 96 in the year's top 100.

As Chapter 1 argued, much of the success of the original film was due to how it fell in line with blockbuster-style filmmaking and high concept marketing techniques emerging in youth cinema at that time. From that point on, *Halloween* closely melded with trends in youth horror, so much so that the success of each *Halloween* film depended on the state of youth horror at the time of its release. Two exceptions are the disappointing releases of 1982's *Halloween III* and Zombie's *Halloween II* in 2009. With the former film, Carpenter and Hill were trying to avoid the slasher film's diminishing returns at the box office—and their creative fatigue with the concept—by moving away from the subgenre, but they were not able to escape the slasher brand name established by the success of the first two films. In the case of *Halloween II*, Zombie's take on the franchise may have grown too abrasive for audiences to handle.

However dissimilar they are, 2018's *Halloween* and 1995's *Curse* illuminate an aspect of the *Halloween* franchise that sets it apart from most other horror franchises: both films illustrate *Halloween*'s *mise en abyme*—its endlessly recurring sequence—of youth. The triad of Laurie, Karen, and Allyson is a reverse-gender reflection of the trans-generational triangle of Tommy, Danny, and infant Stephen in *Curse*. While family tension and trauma are themes that run throughout horror cinema, no other horror franchise focuses on generational tension as exhaustively as the *Halloween* films: Michael chases his sister Laurie and then his niece Jamie, Laurie (as Keri) fights her son John, Michael's stepfather abuses him in the remake, and so on. As this chain winds its way throughout these films, the viewer encounters a metamorphic image of youth. The presence of young adults, teens, preadolescents, and infants suggests the vitality of *Halloween*, a franchise that continues to be reborn.

Conclusion

This chapter examined the *Halloween* franchise and made two principal observations. First, the success or failure of individual films in the *Halloween* franchise suggests the state of youth horror at the time of the film's release. Second, as the franchise has evolved, it has produced a wide array of youth characters and will probably continue to do so as the franchise continues to be reborn and rejuvenate itself. Similar to the original film, sequel logic is built into the conclusion of the 2018 version. As the trio ride along in the truck bed, the camera cranes over and tracks in on Allyson's other hand, which still clutches a bloody knife she grabbed during the fight. Does Allyson still clutch the knife because she somehow intuits that she will need to defend herself when Michael returns? If the *Halloween* franchise's past is any indication of its future, she will. *Halloween* is a resilient franchise, constantly regenerating itself every ten years or so. Each rebirth seems to bring a new timeline that variously designates past entries of the franchise as canonical or apocryphal. Claire Parody writes that for fans of a franchise, 'Shifting between "canons" and narrative realities . . . [is] often a rewarding form of mastery over a franchise text, not a source of tension' (2011: 216).

The *Halloween* franchise provides its followers with this type of experience, with many fans having fun with the franchise's multiple worlds and continuities. On 18 October 2018, *The Horrors of Halloween* blog featured an overview of the different ways in which online fans had attempted to map out the franchise's various timelines. The post featured no fewer than five charts, one of which, created by blogger Marcus Alexander Hart, re-imaged the franchise as a huge 'Choose Your Own Adventure' book, harkening back to the popular children's gamebook series from the 1980s and 1990s that allowed readers to make decisions at key points in the narrative and chart their own course through the fictional world ('Halloween Choose . . .' 2018) (see Figure 4.3). As a franchise that continues to be reborn over and over again, *Halloween* will undoubtedly continue to offer young and adventurous viewers multiple worlds to explore. Some will be familiar; others may be strange. But they will all be infused with an eerie atmosphere that recalls the horror of growing up common to all.

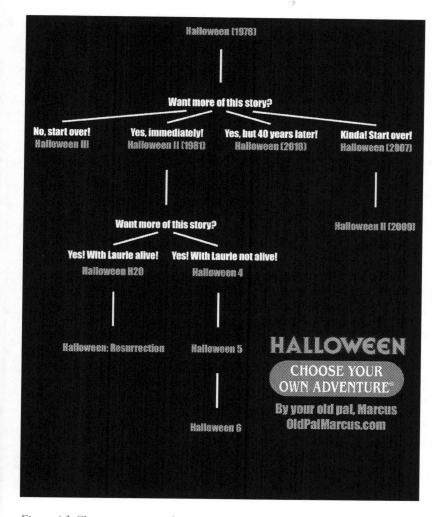

Figure 4.3 Choose your own adventure

Image courtesy of Marcus Alexander Hart, OldPalMarcus.com

Notes

1 Note also the lack of a knife on *Halloween II*'s poster discussed in Chapter 1.
2 From 1990 to 1995, there were around 31 horror films total that broke the top 100 grossing films in the year of their release. Only around eight of these films (counting *Curse*) were slashers. With only a few exceptions, these films placed in the bottom half of the top 100 of their respective years.
3 Trancas preferred a significantly different version of the film, known among fans as 'The Producers Cut.' Dimension and the director preferred a cut that removed some exposition and was more violent and gory. Their version was released theatrically. In 2013, both versions were released on home video by Scream Factory.
4 See Scream Factory (2013).
5 The title of the original 1974 film is *The Texas* **Chain Saw** *Massacre*, but this unique spelling of "chainsaw" has not been retained for any other films in the franchise.
6 Harris played Jamie in *Halloween 4* and *5*, so her casting evokes the franchise's history.
7 An extended version of this scene in Zombie's workprint shows Lynda bullying a couple of students, yelling at them, and pouring a drink on one's head.
8 Grossing $51.5 million and $65 million, respectively.

Bibliography

Altman, R. (1999) *Film/Genre*, London: British Film Institute.

Artz, M. (2017) 'David Gordon Green Describes Pitching His "Halloween" to John Carpenter,' *Halloween Daily News*, online, 7 March, https://halloweendailynews. com/2017/03/david-gordon-green-halloween/ (accessed 14 April 2019).

Assip, M. (2017) 'Exclusive Interview: Denis Etchison on His Unmade Halloween 4 and the Ghosts of the Lost River Drive-In,' *Blumhouse*, online, 6 January, https:// web.archive.org/web/20170108183635/www.blumhouse.com/2017/01/06/ exclusive-interview-dennis-etchison-on-his-unmade-halloween-4-the-ghostsof-the-lost-river-drive-in/ (accessed 14 April 2019).

Bay, A. (2013a) Halloween Blu-ray, Region 1, Audio Commentary with John Carpenter, et al., disc 2.

Bay, A. (2013b) Halloween Blu-ray, Region 1, Halloween: A Cut Above the Rest featurette, disc 2.

Benshoff, H. (2014) 'Horror Before "The Horror Film",' in Benshoff, H. (ed) *A Companion to the Horror Film*, Malden: Wiley-Blackwell, pp. 207–224.

Bernard, M. (2014) *Selling the Splat Pack: The DVD Revolution and the American Horror Film*, Edinburgh: Edinburgh University Press.

Black, G.D. (1994) *Hollywood Censored: Morality Codes, Catholics, and the Movies*, Cambridge: Cambridge University Press.

Boulenger, G. (2001) *John Carpenter: The Prince of Darkness*, Los Angeles: Silman-James.

Bracke, P.M. (2006) *Crystal Lake Memories: The Complete History of Friday the 13th*, London: Titan.

Britton, A. (1979) 'The Exorcist,' in Wood, R. and Lippe, R. (eds) *The American Nightmare: Essays on the Horror Film*, Toronto: Festival of Festivals, pp. 50–54.

Britton, A. (2009) 'Blissing Out: The Politics of Reaganite Entertainment,' in Grant, B.K. (ed) *Britton on Film: The Complete Criticism of Andrew Britton*, Detroit: Wayne State University Press, pp. 97–154.

Browning, J.E. (2014) 'Classical Hollywood Horror,' in Benshoff, H. (ed) *A Companion to the Horror Film*, Malden: Wiley-Blackwell, pp. 225–236.

Carlomagno, E. (1982) 'Halloween III: Season of the Witch,' *Fangoria*, 3:22, pp. 8–12.

Carpenter, J. (2013) Interview with Murray Leeder, 25 August.

Clover, C.J. (1987) 'Her Body, Himself: Gender in the Slasher Film,' *Representations*, 20, Fall, pp. 187–228.

Clover, C.J. (2015) 'Her Body, Himself: Gender in the Slasher Film,' in Grant, B.K. (ed) *The Dread of Difference: Gender and the Horror Film*, 2nd ed., Austin: University of Texas Press, pp. 68–115.

Conrich, I. (2019) 'John Carpenter,' *Oxford Bibliographies*, online, 24 April, www.oxfordbibliographies.com/view/document/obo-9780199791286/obo-9780199791286-0317.xml?rskey=lJIEoK&result=45 (assessed 22 May 2019).

Conrich, I. and D. Woods (2004) 'Introduction,' in Conrich, I. and Woods, D. (eds) *John Carpenter: The Technique of Terror*, New York: Wallflower, pp. 1–9.

Cook, D.A. (2000) *Lost Illusions: American Cinema in the Shadow of Watergate and Vietnam, 1970–1979*, Berkeley: University of California Press.

Cook, D.A. (2007) '1974: Movies and Political Trauma,' in Friedman, L. (ed) *American Cinema of the 1970s: Themes and Variations*, New Brunswick: Rutgers University Press, pp. 116–134.

Cook, D.A. (2016) *A History of Narrative Cinema*, 5th ed., New York: W.W. Norton.

Cumbow, R.C. (2000) *Order in the Universe: The Films of John Carpenter*, 2nd ed., Lanham: Scarecrow.

Davis, B. (2012) *Battle for the Bs: 1950s Hollywood and the Rebirth of Low-Budget Cinema*, New Brunswick: Rutgers University Press.

'Defining Carpenteresque' (2018) Through the Lens, online, IMDb Originals.

Dika, V. (1990) *Games of Terror: Halloween, Friday the 13th, and the Films of the Slasher Cycle*, Vancouver: Fairleigh Dickinson University Press.

Dixon, W.W. (2010) *A History of Horror*, New Brunswick: Rutgers University Press.

Doherty, T. (1999) *Pre-Code Hollywood: Sex, Immorality, and Insurrection in American Cinema, 1930–1934*, New York: Columbia University Press.

Doherty, T. (2002) *Teenagers and Teenpics: The Juvenilization of American Movies in the 1950s*, Philadelphia: Temple University Press.

Draper, E. (1999) '"Controversy Has Probably Destroyed Forever the Context": The Miracle and Movie Censorship in America in the 1950s,' in Bernstein, M. (ed) *Controlling Hollywood: Censorship and Regulation in the Studio Era*, New Brunswick: Rutgers University Press, pp. 186–205.

Forman-Brunell, M. (2002) 'Maternity, Murder, and Monsters: Legends of Babysitter Horror,' in Gateward, F. and Pomerance, M. (eds) *Sugar, Spice, and Everything Nice: Cinemas of Girlhood*, Detroit: Wayne State University Press, pp. 253–268.

'Franchises: Halloween' (no date) Box Office Mojo, online, www.boxofficemojo.com/franchises/chart/?id=halloween.htm/ (accessed 17 May 2019).

Grant, B.K. (2004) 'Disorder in the Universe: John Carpenter and the Question of Genre,' in Conrich, I. and Woods, D. (eds) *John Carpenter: The Technique of Terror*, New York: Wallflower, pp. 10–20.

Gray, B. (2004) *Roger Corman: An Unauthorized Life*, New York: Thunder's Mouth.

Hall, S. (2004) 'Carpenter's Widescreen Style,' in Conrich, I. and Woods, D. (eds) *John Carpenter: The Technique of Terror*, New York: Wallflower, pp. 66–77.

'Halloween' (1990) Fangoria Presents Best & Bloodiest Horror Video, 2, pp. 36–37.

'Halloween 5' (1990) Fangoria Presents Best & Bloodiest Horror Video, 2, p. 37.

'Halloween Choose Your Own Adventure, Times, Sequels Explained' (2018) The Horrors of Halloween, online, 18 October, www.thehorrorsofhalloween.com/2018/10/halloween-choose-your-adventure-timelines-sequels-explained.html/ (accessed 12 April 2019).

Heffernan, K. (2004) *Ghouls, Gimmicks, and Gold: Horror Films and the American Movie Business, 1953–1968*, Durham: Duke University Press.

Humphries, R. (2002) *The American Horror Film: An Introduction*, Edinburgh: Edinburgh University Press.

Hutchings, P. (2013) *The Horror Film*, New York: Routledge.

Hutchings, P. (2014a) 'By the Book: American Horror Cinema and Horror Literature of the Late 1960s and 1970s,' in Nowell, R. (ed) *Merchants of Menace: The Business of Horror Cinema*, New York: Bloomsbury, pp. 45–60.

Hutchings, P. (2014b) 'International Horror in the 1970s,' in Benshoff, H. (ed) *A Companion to the Horror Film*, Malden: Wiley-Blackwell, pp. 292–309.

'ITC Serif Gothic' (no date) FontShop, online, www.fontshop.com/families/adobe-itc-serif-gothic/(accessed 14 April 2019).

Jameson, R.T. (2009) 'Review: Halloween,' *Parallax View*, online, 30 October, https://parallax-view.org/2009/10/30/review-halloween (accessed 14 April 2019).

Jameson, R.T. (2012) 'Style Vs. "Style",' *Queen Anne and Magnolia News*, online, 4 September, https://queenannenews.com/Content/Straight-Shooting/Straight-Shooting/Article/Style-vs-Style-/83/399/33351/ (accessed 14 April 2019).

Jancovich, M. (1996) *Rational Fears: American Horror in the 1950s*, Manchester: Manchester University Press.

Jancovich, M. (2014) 'Horror in the 1940s,' in Benshoff, H. (ed) *A Companion to the Horror Film*, Malden: Wiley-Blackwell, pp. 237–254.

Jess-Cooke, C. (2009) *Film Sequels: Theory and Practice From Hollywood to Bollywood*, Edinburgh: Edinburgh University Press.

Kearney, M.C. (2002) 'Girlfriends and Girl Power: Female Adolescence in Contemporary U.S. Cinema,' in Gateward, F. and Pomerance, M. (eds) *Sugar, Spice, and Everything Nice: Cinemas of Girlhood*, Detroit: Wayne State University Press, pp. 125–144.

Kendrick, J. (2014) 'Slasher Films and Gore in the 1980s,' in Benshoff, H. (ed) *A Companion to the Horror Film*, Malden: Wiley-Blackwell, pp. 310–328.

Klein, B. (2018) 'Brennan Went to Film School: In Defense of Halloween: Resurrection,' *Dread Central*, online, 18 October, www.dreadcentral.com/news/283892/brennan-went-to-film-school-in-defense-of-halloween-resurrection/ (accessed 14 April 2019).

Koven, M.J. (2008) *Film, Folklore and Urban Legends*, Lanham: Scarecrow.

Leeder, M. (2014) *Halloween*, Leighton Buzzard: Auteur.

Lewis, J. (2000) *Hollywood v. Hardcore: How the Struggle Over Censorship Created the Modern Film Industry*, New York: New York University Press.

Lewis, J. (2003) 'Following the Money in America's Sunniest Company Town: Some Notes on the Political Economy of the Hollywood Blockbuster,' in Stringer, J. (ed) *Movie Blockbusters*, New York: Routledge, pp. 61–71.

Maltby, R. (2003) *Hollywood Cinema*, 2nd ed., Malden: Blackwell.

Marriott, J. and K. Newman (2010) *Horror! 333 Films to Scare You to Death*, London: Carlton.

Mathijs, E. (2009) 'Threat or Treat: Film, Television, and the Ritual of Halloween,' *Flow*, online, 30 October, www.flowjournal.org/2009/10/threat-or-treat-film-television-and-the-ritual-of-halloween-ernest-mathijs-the-university-of-british-columbia/ (accessed 14 April 2019).

Mathijs, E. and J. Sexton (2011) *Cult Cinema: An Introduction*, Malden: Wiley-Blackwell.

McCarthy, T. (1980) 'Treat and Treat: John Carpenter Interviewed by Todd McCarthy,' *Film Comment*, 16:1, pp. 17–24.

Meehan, E.R. (1991) '"Holy Commodity Fetish, Batman!": The Political Economy of a Commercial Intertext,' in Pearson, R. and Uricchio, W. (eds) *The Many Lives of the Batman: Critical Approaches to a Superhero and His Media*, New York, Routledge, pp. 47–65.

Miska, B. (2015) '"Halloween" Shocker: Dimension No Longer Controlling Michael Myers?! (Exclusive),' *Bloody Disgusting*, online, 28 December, https://bloody-disgusting.com/exclusives/3374609/halloween-shocker-dimension-no-longer-controlling-michael-myers-exclusive/ (accessed 17 May 2019).

Muir, J.K. (2000) *The Films of John Carpenter*, Jefferson: McFarland.

Neale, S. (2004) 'Halloween: Suspense, Aggression, and the Look,' in Grant, B.K (ed) *Planks of Reason: Essays on the Horror Film*, Revised ed., Lanham: Scarecrow, pp. 356–369.

Nelson, A.P. (2010) 'Traumatic Childhood Now Included: Todorov's Fantastic and the Uncanny Slasher Remake,' in Hantke, S. (ed) *American Horror Film: The Genre at the Turn of the Millennium*, Jackson: University Press of Mississippi, pp. 119–132.

Nichols, D.P. (1980) 'Fade to Black,' *Fangoria*, 2:8, pp. 14–15, 41–42.

Nowell, R. (2011) *Blood Money: A History of the First Teen Slasher Film Cycle*, New York: Continuum.

Parody, C. (2011) 'Franchising/Adaptation,' *Adaptation*, 4:2, July, pp. 210–218.

Paul, W. (1994) *Laughing Screaming: Modern Hollywood Horror and Comedy*, New York: Columbia University Press.

Peary, D. (1981) *Cult Movies: The Classics, the Sleepers, the Weird, and the Wonderful*, New York: Delta.

Pimentel, D. (2013) 'The Widening Maturity Gap: Trying and Punishing Juveniles as Adults in an Era of Extended Adolescence,' *Texas Tech Law Review*, 46:1, pp. 71–102.

Polan, D. (2007) *Scenes of Instruction: The Beginnings of the U.S. Study of Film*, Berkeley: University of California Press.

Proctor, W. (2012) 'Regeneration and Rebirth: An Anatomy of the Franchise Reboot,' *Scope: An Online Journal of Film and Television Studies*, 22, February, pp. 1–19.

Roche, D. (2014) *Making and Remaking Horror in the 1970s and 2000s: Why Don't They Do It Like They Used To?* Jackson: University Press of Mississippi.

Rockoff, A. (2002) *Going to Pieces: The Rise and Fall of the Slasher Film, 1978–1986*, Jefferson: McFarland.

Rosenbaum, J. (1979) 'Halloween (1979 Review),' *Jonathan Rosenbaum*, online, 30 January, www.jonathanrosenbaum.net/1979/01/halloween-1979-review/ (accessed 14 April 2019).

Schatz, T. (1981) *Hollywood Genres: Formulas, Filmmaking, and the Studio System*, New York: McGraw-Hill.

Schatz, T. (2003) 'The New Hollywood,' in Stringer, J. (ed) *Movie Blockbusters*, New York: Routledge, pp. 15–44.

Scream Factory (2013) 'Halloween H20: Twenty Years Later Blu-ray, Region 1,' *The Making of Halloween H20* featurette, disc 1.

Shary, T. (2005) *Teen Movies: American Youth on Screen*, New York: Wallflower.

Shary, T. (2014) *Generation Multiplex: The Image of Youth in American Cinema Since 1980*, 2nd ed., Austin: University of Texas Press.

Short, S. (2007) *Misfit Sisters: Screen Horror as Female Rites of Passage*, Hampshire: Palgrave Macmillan.

Skal, D.J. (1993) *The Monster Show: A Cultural History of Horror*, New York: Penguin.

Smith, S. (2004) 'A Siege Mentality? Form and Ideology in Carpenter's Early Siege Films,' in Conrich, I. and Woods, D. (eds) *John Carpenter: The Technique of Terror*, New York: Wallflower, pp. 35–48.

Sprague, M. (2018) 'Halloween Beats Scream as Highest Grossing Slasher Film Ever,' *Dread Central*, online, 29 October, www.dreadcentral.com/news/284623/halloween-beats-scream-as-highest-grossing-slasher-film-ever/ (accessed 14 April 2019).

Stetka, B. (2017) 'Extended Adolescence: When 25 Is the New 18,' *Scientific American*, online, 19 September, www.scientificamerican.com/article/extended-adolescence-when-25-is-the-new-18/ (accessed 14 April 2019).

Telotte, J.P. (1987) 'Through a Pumpkin's Eye: The Reflexive Nature of Horror,' in Waller, G. (ed) *American Horrors: Essays on the Modern American Horror Film*, Champaign: University of Illinois Press, pp. 114–128.

Tudor, A. (1989) *Monsters and Mad Scientists: A Cultural History of the Horror Movie*, Oxford: Basil Blackwell.

Tudor, A. (2002) 'From Paranoia to Postmodernism? The Horror Movie in Late Modern Society,' in Neale, S. (ed) *Genre and Contemporary Hollywood*, London: British Film Institute, pp. 105–116.

Tzioumakis, Y. (2017) *American Independent Cinema: An Introduction*, 2nd ed., Edinburgh: Edinburgh University Press.

Vasey, R. (1997) *The World According to Hollywood, 1918–1939*, Madison: University of Wisconsin Press.

Walpole, H. (2014) *The Castle of Otranto*, Oxford: Oxford University Press.

Weaver, T., et al. (2007) *Universal Horrors: The Studio's Classic Films, 1931–1946*, 2nd ed., Jefferson: McFarland.

Williamson, M. (2005) *The Lure of the Vampire: Gender, Fiction, and Fandom From Bram Stoker to Buffy*, New York: Wallflower.

Wood, R. (1979a) 'An Introduction to the American Horror Film,' in Wood, R. and Lippe, R. (eds) *The American Nightmare: Essays on the Horror Film*, Toronto: Festival of Festivals, pp. 7–28.

Wood, R. (1979b) 'Sisters,' in Wood, R. and Lippe, R. (eds) *The American Nightmare: Essays on the Horror Film*, Toronto: Festival of Festivals, pp. 59–63.

Wood, R. (1979c) 'World of Gods and Monsters: The Films of Larry Cohen,' in Wood, R. and Lippe, R. (eds) *The American Nightmare: Essays on the Horror Film*, Toronto: Festival of Festivals, pp. 74–86.

Wood, R. (1983) 'Cronenberg: A Dissenting View,' in Handling, P. (ed) *The Shape of Rage: The Films of David Cronenberg*, Toronto: General, pp. 115–135.

Wood, R. (1986) *Hollywood From Vietnam to Reagan*, New York: Columbia University Press.

Wood, R. and Lippe, R. (eds) (1979) *The American Nightmare: Essays on the Horror Film*, Toronto: Festival of Festivals.

Woods, D. (2004) 'Us and Them: Authority and Identity in Carpenter's Films,' in Conrich, I. and Woods, D. (eds) *John Carpenter: The Technique of Terror*, New York: Wallflower, pp. 21–34.

Worland, R. (2007) *The Horror Film: An Introduction*, Malden: Blackwell.

Wyatt, J. (1994) *High Concept: Movies and Marketing in Hollywood*, Austin: University of Texas Press.

Yablans, I. (2012) *The Man Who Created Halloween*, Lexington: CreateSpace.

Zinoman, J. (2011) *Shock Value: How a Few Eccentric Outsiders Gave Us Nightmares, Conquered Hollywood, and Invented Modern Horror*, New York: Penguin.

Index

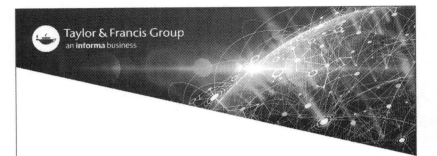

Printed in the United States
by Baker & Taylor Publisher Services